HISPANIC TEXTS

general editor Professor Peter Beardsell
  Department of Hispanic Studies, University of Hull

series previously edited by Emeritus Professor Herbert Ramsden

series adviser Catherine Davies
  Department of Spanish and Portuguese Studies, University of Manchester

Hispanic Texts provide important and attractive material in editions with an introduction, notes and vocabulary, and are suitable both for advanced study in schools, colleges and higher education and for use by the general reader. Continuing the tradition established by the previous *Spanish Texts*, the series combines a high standard of scholarship with practical linguistic assistance for English speakers. It aims to respond to recent changes in the kind of text selected for study, or chosen as background reading to support the acquisition of foreign languages, and places an emphasis on modern texts which not only deserve attention in their own right but contribute to a fuller understanding of the societies in which they were written. While many of these works are regarded as modern classics, others are included for their suitability as useful and enjoyable reading material, and may contain colloquial and journalistic as well as literary Spanish. The series will also give fuller representation to the increasing literary, political and economic importance of Latin America.

La casa de Bernarda Alba

MANCHESTER
UNIVERSITY PRESS

D1370614

HISPANIC TEXTS

also available

Julio Cortázar *Siete cuentos*
 ed. Peter Beardsell

Carlos Fuentes *Agua Quemada: cuarteto narrativo*
 ed. Steven Boldy

José Luis Olaizola *La guerra del general Escobar*
 ed. Rosemary Clark

Short fiction by Spanish American women
 ed. Evelyn Fishburn

La vida de Lazarillo de Tormes
 ed. R. O. Jones

Antonio Buero Vallejo *La doble historia del Doctor Valmy*
 ed. Barry Jordan

Miguel de Unamuno *San Manuel Bueno, mártir* and *La novela de don Sandalio*
 ed. C. A. Longhurst

Ramón J. Sender *Réquiem por un campesino español*
 ed. Patricia McDermott

Gabriel García Márquez *El coronel no tiene quien le escriba*
 ed. Giovanni Pontiero

Federico García Lorca *Bodas de sangre*
 ed. H. Ramsden

Federico García Lorca *Romancero gitano*
 ed. H. Ramsden

Federico García Lorca *Yerma*
 ed. Robin Warner

Frederico García Lorca

La casa de Bernarda Alba

edited with introduction, notes and vocabulary by

H. Ramsden
Emeritus Professor at the University of Manchester

Manchester University Press
Manchester and New York

distributed exclusively in the USA and Canada by St. Martin's Press

Published by Manchester University Press
Oxford Road, Manchester M13 9NR, UK
and Room 400, 175 Fifth Avenue, New York, NY 10010, USA

Distributed exclusively in the USA by
St. Martin's Press, Inc., 175 Fifth Avenue, New York, NY 10010, USA

Distributed exclusively in Canada by
UBC Press, University of British Columbia, 6344 Memorial Road, Vancouver, BC, Canada V6T 1Z2

British Library Cataloguing-in-Publication Data
A catalogue record for this book is available from the British Library

Library of Congress Cataloging-in-Publication Data applied for

ISBN 0 7190 0950 2 *paperback*

First published 1983

06   05   04   03   02   01   00   12   11   10   9   8   7   6

Printed in Great Britain
by BPC Wheatons Ltd, Exeter

CONTENTS

PREFACE   vi

INTRODUCTION   vii

    Preliminaries   vii
    An Outline of the Play   ix
    Vitality and Repression   xv
    Realism and Poetry   xxix
    'La obra más perfecta'?   lv

SELECTED BIBLIOGRAPHY   lxi

LA CASA DE BERNARDA ALBA   1

    Acto primero   3
    Acto segundo   34
    Acto tercero   67

ENDNOTES   92

SELECTED VOCABULARY   96

PREFACE

The present edition is aimed primarily at sixth-formers and university undergraduates. The reception accorded to my edition of *Bodas de sangre* encourages me to hope that it will also be of more specialist interest.

The timing of the edition has been fortunate, for I have been able to base my text on the manuscript version of the play recently published by Mario Hernández (Alianza, Madrid 1981). This reveals over three hundred differences from the Losada first edition of 1945 on which, albeit with changes, all editions to 1981 were based. Most of these differences are insignificant and add nothing to our appreciation of the text; others are minor but, taken together, give a superior text to that traditionally accepted and effectively out-date previous editions; finally, in a few cases the differences are striking and important. In my own edition I have departed from the Hernández text only on a few minor points, principally of punctu-ation, where I have preferred the Losada or Aguilar reading, and on one more important point where I depart from all existing editions (Endnote H). Given the aims of the Spanish Texts Series — and extreme limitations of space — I have in general not sought to justify these preferences but have drawn attention in notes to some of the more striking differences between the manuscript version and the traditional text. Mario Hernández's manuscript editions represent the most exciting advance in current Lorca scholarship and I am pleased to express my indebtedness to his edition of *La casa de Bernarda Alba*.

Thanks are due also, at a more modest level, to my 1981–2 first-year Honours students who guided me closely in the selection of vocabulary and notes. Finally, I am indebted to Doña Isabel García Lorca and to New Directions for allowing me to publish this edition and to the Manchester University Press and their printers for much care in its preparation.

1983   H.R.

INTRODUCTION

PRELIMINARIES

Lorca completed the existing manuscript of *La casa de Bernarda Alba* on 19 June 1936, read it to friends a few days later and expressed his hope that the play would be staged in the autumn, probably in October.[1] On 16 July, two days before the outbreak of the Spanish Civil War, he departed for Granada to spend the summer as usual with his family, was arrested in Granada on 16 August and executed three days later on the order of the Civil Governor. The play was premiered in Buenos Aires on 8 March 1945. Amidst general press silence it was first produced in Madrid in 1950 by the intimate theatre group La Carátula. In 1963 it was produced by Juan Antonio Bardem for the larger commercial stage.

Little is known about the chronology of writing. Lorca tended to take several years maturing a play in his mind ('un pensar largo, constante, enjundioso', II, 1047) and then to write it fairly quickly. In an interview given in 1933 he described *Bodas de sangre* as 'la parte primera de una trilogía dramática de la tierra española', said he was working on the second part, on the theme of the barren woman, and announced that the third part, *La destrucción de Sodoma*, was 'madurando ahora dentro de mi corazón' (II, 962). In the following year, shortly before the premiere of *Yerma*, Lorca mentioned his trilogy again, referring to the third part as *El drama de las hijas de Loth* (II, 1036). In 1935 he again used the title *La destrucción de Sodoma* (II, 1038). He was clearly referring to the same play (cf. Genesis xix) and Martínez Nadal has recalled Lorca's account of the plot.[2] This confirms what the titles suggest: that despite some similarity between the dilemma of Lot's daughters ('there is not a man in the earth to come unto us after the manner of all the earth',

[1] Carlos Morla Lynch, *En España con Federico García Lorca*, Aguilar, Madrid 1958, pp. 483–9.

[2] Rafael Martínez Nadal, *El público*, Dolphin, Oxford 1970, pp. 13–14. See also Suzanne Byrd, who reconstructs the play from a different source, in *García Lorca Review* 4 (1976), 105–8.

Genesis xix, 31) and that of Bernarda's daughters, *La casa de Bernarda Alba* cannot be seen simply as a revision of *El drama de las hijas de Loth*, though it may of course be a substitution, thus completing the intended trilogy.

This possibility is considered by Allen Josephs and Juan Caballero in their edition of the play but is rejected on two grounds: first, that there is a notable stylistic difference between *Bodas de sangre* and *Yerma* on the one hand and *La casa de Bernarda Alba* on the other, and secondly, that Lorca himself referred repeatedly to the first two plays as 'tragedias' and to the last as a 'drama' (see Selected Bibliography, *21*, 44–9, 69–71). But Josephs and Caballero overlook two important pieces of evidence: (1) according to Lorca's brother, one of the first to emphasise the stylistic difference between the plays, Lorca himself said that with *La casa de Bernarda Alba* 'he closed the cycle, gathered in this trilogy, of rural dramas';[3] (2) even in the trilogy as originally planned Lorca referred to his third play as a drama, *El drama de las hijas de Loth*, and therefore, apparently, saw no objection to including both tragedy and drama in the same trilogy. Add to this that the three plays that we now know all fit nicely under Lorca's own heading, 'tierra española' (II, 962), and that stylistically *Yerma* can be shown to lie between *Bodas de sangre* and *La casa de Bernarda Alba*, and there seems little doubt that this last play was in fact a substitute for the 'grave y comprometedor' treatment of incest that the earlier biblical titles suggest (II, 1038) and that it therefore completes the trilogy. This does not mean that the three plays necessarily constitute a trilogy of the sort that one associates with Greek tragedy. It does, however, seem probable that with the incorporation of *La casa de Bernarda Alba* the trilogy became thematically more unified than it would have been as originally planned and therefore, in this respect at least, that it came closer to the Greek concept of a trilogy.

In the belief that *La casa de Bernarda Alba* does form part of the

---

[3] Francisco García Lorca, Introduction to *Lorca, Three Tragedies*, Penguin (1947), pp. 27–8. See also another well-qualified observer, Carlos Morla Lynch, who was present at the first reading of the play, described it in his diary and, presumably prompted by Lorca, referred to 'esa trilogía que forman *Bodas de sangre, Yerma* y *La casa de Bernarda Alba*' (*op. cit.*, p. 487).

same trilogy as *Bodas de sangre* and *Yerma* I shall make occasional brief comparative references in what follows to *Bodas de sangre* to bring out similarities and differences, but shall reserve comparisons with *Yerma* for my forthcoming edition of this play. Given the necessary brevity of my introduction I shall emphasise two basic problems: first, that of the dramatic conflict involved, which I believe throws light on the much discussed question of Lorca's social commitment; secondly, that of realism and poetry. In each case I shall break down the general problem into simpler component parts so that they can be better studied.

But a work of art is above all a synthesis. Before proceeding to analyse I therefore start with an outline of the play and emphasise the overall dramatic progression.

AN OUTLINE OF THE PLAY

Act I

The title of the play suggests the special relevance of Bernarda's house and the curtain rises on an inner room. The initial absence of characters on stage concentrates attention on the setting, and the stage directions should be considered closely. Against a brooding background of silence church bells toll sombrely.

Poncia and the Criada reveal the most relevant circumstances: the death of Bernarda's second husband, the family's standing in the area, the composition and situation of the family, and Bernarda's odiously authoritarian character. In part at least Bernarda represents the pinnacle of a firmly structured and singularly uncharitable domestic hierarchy: she drives Poncia, Poncia drives the Criada and, as we see a moment later, the Criada vents her authority and bad temper on the woman who comes begging for scraps of food.

When the village women have gathered in tribute to the dead man Bernarda appears with her five daughters. Within thirty seconds she confirms most of what Poncia has said of her: she is domineering ('¡Silencio! Menos gritos y más obras'; cf. '¡Mandona! ¡Dominanta!'), much preoccupied with cleanliness ('Debías haber procurado que todo esto estuviera más limpio'; cf. 'Ella la más aseada') and arrogantly superior ('Los pobres son como los animales.

Parece como si estuvieran hechos de otras sustancias'; cf. 'ella la más alta') — to which is added, shortly afterwards, evidence of her sensitivity to criticism and of her viciousness in criticizing others ('Estaba su madre ... el calor de la pana'; cf. 'ella la más decente', 'días enteros mirando por la rendija para espiar a los vecinos y llevarle el cuento'). These parallels between what Poncia said and what Bernarda herself reveals serve to impress the characteristics on the audience. They also serve to establish Poncia as a reliable guide to the action of the play.

The litany for the dead husband offers a striking contrast to so much nastiness and suggests that formalised religion has little to do with charity. As the neighbours depart, Bernarda affirms that the house will return to its isolation ('¡Ojalá tardéis mucho años en pasar el arco de mi puerta! [...] En ocho años que dure el luto ...'; cf. 'Desde que murió el padre de Bernarda no han vuelto a entrar las gentes bajo estos techos'). Meanwhile the girls can embroider their trousseaus. It is a typical Lorcan situation: on the one hand, the object of the needlework, in this case marriage, a possible outlet for female vitality; on the other hand, the needlework itself, a pointer to female repression. But Magdalena, the second daughter, says she has no illusions about marriage; she wishes only to escape, a wish that is immediately taken up by the grandmother off stage. As the Criada goes off to let the grandmother out, Bernarda learns of Angustias's eavesdropping on the men outside and angrily summons her daughter and strikes her. The men were talking about sexual adventures with Paca la Roseta. It is all part of a gradual build-up of threatening male vitality outside the house, countered by Bernarda with restrictions on her daughters' activities and the denial to four of them of both *novios* and marriage. The *muros gruesos* of the setting — and the apparent lack of windows — seem increasingly relevant. So do the pictures on the wall (cf. Magdalena's finding of escape and consolation in such pictures, 24). Adela, the youngest daughter, has put on her green dress (a threat of revolt amidst so much black and white) and responds with tears of anger to news of Pepe el Romano's expected marriage to Angustias. Male vitality, then, has been given specific form and the daughters go off excitedly to spy on Pepe as he comes along the street. News of the dead man's will and of Angustias's specially favoured position has not lessened Bernarda's determination to rule her house absolutely and she again attacks Angustias for immodest behaviour. 'Madre, déjeme usted salir', pleads the daughter, and a moment later her plea is echoed by the crazy María Josefa who has escaped from her room and appears decked out in flowers (another image of revolt): ' ¡Déjame salir, Bernarda! '. But María Josefa, in her madness, is more specific than her granddaughters have dared to be: 'yo quiero un varón para casarme y tener alegría', and this is immediately countered by Bernarda's ' ¡Encerradla! ' (the *muros gruesos* again). It is the clearest expression so far of the conflict between vitality and repression that has run through the act. Emotivity of speech (exclamations, imperatives, contrast, repetition) and violence of action (another manifestation of emotion) serve to emphasize the point. Even the final *telón* seems involved as it descends rapidly to stifle María Josefa's clamour for escape.

Act II

In another inner room, again apparently without windows, the daughters are sewing. The increased bitterness of their relationship is accompanied by references to the oppressive heat and a threatening storm, and fresh air is sought by opening the door to the patio. There are unresolved doubts about Pepe's visit the night before, ostensibly to court Angustias, and Adela is unwell. Tension is relieved momentarily by Poncia's earthy account of her own courtship and marriage, but the bitterness returns with Adela's appearance and it is centred on Angustias's expected marriage. When the four older daughters go off to examine lace brought by a travelling vendor, Poncia probes Adela about her relationship with Pepe and prompts a defiant declaration of love and desire. Nor is it only love and desire from a distance. 'Mirando sus ojos me parece que bebo su sangre lentamente.' For the audience at least there can no longer be much doubt about the unexplained hours of Pepe's visit.

When Martirio, Amelia and Magdalena return there is further bickering and bitterness, interrupted moments later by a joyful sound of bells *'como a través de varios muros'* as the men outside return to the fields. The contrast is evident and it is heightened by references to the joy of the countryside at this time of year, the joy and vitality of the newly arrived reapers, and by the singing and playing of the reapers themselves. Adela, **Magdalena** and Poncia go off to spy on the men from a bedroom window and Martirio and Amelia return to the subject of unexplained nocturnal activity in the farmyard.

Angustias bursts in, angry at the disappearance of Pepe's photo from under her pillow, and is followed immediately by Adela, Magdalena and Poncia. All the daughters disclaim responsibility and amidst increasing clamour Bernarda herself appears, imposes silence and has the rooms searched. To Poncia's surprise — for the torment of sexual repression is greater than even she had realised — the photo is found in Martirio's bed. During the beating and the passions that follow, Martirio proclaims — to no one's conviction — that it was only a joke. 'Yo veía la tormenta venir', says Bernarda, 'pero no creía que estallara tan pronto.' As she dismisses her daughters, she resolves on even stricter control. Poncia tries to reason with her, but as a servant in an authoritarian household, 'una extraña en el centro de la familia' — despite thirty years' service —, she is necessarily oblique in her approach. Her observations do, however, coincide with what the audience itself has been made to see: the daughters' natural desires, the incitement offered by Pepe el Romano, Bernarda's excessive repression, the unsuitability of the proposed marriage, and the need to clarify conflicting reports about the time and extent of Pepe's visits. With public reputation as her norm Bernarda responds both defensively ('ha sido una broma'; 'Aquí no pasa nada') and aggressively (with abusive references to Poncia's mother and origin). She is unable to understand that a servant, too, may be concerned for the well-being of the family for which she works and be anxious to uphold its reputation. Poncia, she believes, desires only the family's downfall (' ¡Cómo gozarías de vernos a mí y a mis hijas camino del lupanar! ') and the destruction of Bernarda's own peace of mind ('Te deslizas para llenarme de malos sueños'). Arrogance and persecution mania, then, go hand in hand and it is significantly Adela's appeal to both these sentiments ('Madre, no oiga usted a quien nos quiere perder a todas') that finally causes Bernarda to set Poncia's warning aside as though the only grounds for it were slanderous gossip:

¡Ya sabré enterarme! Si las gentes del pueblo quieren levantar falsos testimonios se encontrarán con mi pedernal. No se hable de este asunto. Hay a veces una ola de fango que levantan los demás para perdernos.

'Has visto lo malo de las gentes a cien leguas', said Poncia to Bernarda a few moments ago; 'Pero los hijos son los hijos. Ahora estás ciega' (58). And again, when faced with Bernarda's insistence that the taking of the photo was only a joke: 'Se trata de lo tuyo. Pero si fuera la vecina de enfrente, ¿qué sería?' (58). Since then Bernarda's blindness towards her own family has been amply illustrated. In the rest of the scene we are shown the other side. The maid comes in with news of a crowd in the street and Poncia is sent off to investigate. After an important exchange between Adela and Martirio on their rival love for Pepe, Poncia returns with news that La Librada's unmarried daughter has had a child and has killed it to hide her shame. The body has been found and the mob is dragging the mother through the streets. The scene ends with Bernarda, supported by Martirio, urging them on to kill her, and with Adela, clutching her own belly, pleading for her to be spared. It is obviously comparable to the end of Act I: emotive speech (exclamations, imperatives, contrast, repetition) and violent action, complementing one another in a climactic juxtaposition of vitality and repression.

Act III

As at the beginning of Act II the audience returns from the interval to a scene that contrasts sharply with the impassioned ending of the previous act. Characters are seated, this time in an inner patio, and a number of highlighted elements — an oil lamp amidst the *perfecta simplicidad* of the setting, the clatter of knives amidst the surrounding *gran silencio* — help to bring out the down-to-earth context of a family meal. But the conversation soon turns to parent—daughter relationships, and a stallion kicking at the wall recalls the threat of male vitality outside. Adela is brought water for her thirst and the conversation shifts to the approaching wedding of Pepe and Angustias, with references to traditional symbols of ill omen. A visiting neighbour leaves and Adela goes off for a breath of fresh air at the doorway to the yard, accompanied by Amelia and Martirio. In a conversation with her mother Angustias expresses concern about Pepe's inattentiveness during his visits, as though he were thinking of something else. One should not probe such things, says Bernarda, a view that coincides exactly with her emphasis, a moment before, on the need for 'buena fachada' within her own household

(73) and contrasts with Poncia's earlier advice, '¡Cuida de enterarte!' (62). Related contrasts between the daughters follow: most notably between Martirio, who is interested only in the circumscribed world of humans, and Adela, who thrills to the mystery of the stars and the freshness of the open countryside.

Pepe is apparently not coming tonight and one by one the daughters go off to bed, followed by Bernarda, confident that the situation is now under control. Left behind, Poncia and Criada comment on the dangers and on Bernarda's arrogant blindness to them. Things have gone too far, says Poncia. Barking dogs suggest that someone is near the gate and Adela appears in her underclothes, allegedly because she is thirsty again and has come for a drink of water. As they all go off, leaving the scene in near darkness, María Josefa comes in nursing a lamb and clamouring again for escape to the 'orilla del mar', associated now with the nativity crib and motherhood. Adela slips across the stage and out through the door to the yard, followed by Martirio who is confronted by María Josefa, with further emphasis on escape and motherhood, and contrasting references to the fate of her granddaughters. As in Acts I and II, characters' movements and passions are becoming more and more agitated as the scene progresses. An impassioned confrontation between Adela and Martirio in which both confess their longing for Pepe is interrupted by Bernarda. But Adela now is in open revolt and breaks Bernarda's stick. Poncia and the remaining daughters appear. Physical movement and violence are accompanied by increasingly emotive and exclamatory speech. Angustias restrains Adela as Bernarda seizes a gun and goes out in pursuit of Pepe. A shot is heard and Martirio announces Pepe's death. Adela dashes off in despair and locks herself in. When Poncia finally forces the door, Adela is found hanged. Bernarda, true to character, responds with thoughts of reputation and with an imposed wall of silence. Blind to the realities of life, she now demands that one should be openeyed to the reality of death.

VITALITY AND REPRESSION

As can be seen from the above outline, the action of the play is centred on a conflict between vitality and repression: on the one hand, the daughters seek an outlet for their vitality through contact with the dynamic world outside; on the other hand, Bernarda tries to repress this vitality by isolating her daughters from such contact.

A Lorcan Constant

One finds a similar conflict in almost all Lorca's works, including his earliest poem (II, 1021) and *Impresiones y paisajes* (1918), a prose work that he wrote and published while still in his teens. Traditionally, he says, monasteries and convents are seen as realms of peace and calm, but I see them as 'teatros de tormentos' and 'desiertos del dolor' (I, 859) where the 'pasiones admirables' of young people struggle with the restraints of their religious vocation (cf. I, 945–6). In the context of a study of *La casa de Bernarda Alba* the following lines are especially relevant – for the theme of vitality and repression, for the contrasting elements through which it is expressed (akin to those in *La casa de Bernarda Alba*) and because Bernarda's house itself is at one point described as a 'convento' (46):

> ¡Qué silencio tan abrumador! Todos ven así el silencio cartujano: paz y tranquilidad. Yo solo veo la inquietud, desasosiego, pasión formidable que late como un enorme corazón por estos claustros. El alma siente deseos de amar, de amar locamente, y deseos de otra alma que se funda con la nuestra..., deseos de gritar, de llorar, de llamar a aquellos infelices que meditan en las celdas, para decirles que hay sol, y luna, y mujeres, y música; de llamarlos para que se despierten para hacer bien por su alma, que está en las tinieblas de la oración, y cantarles algo muy optimista y agradable..., pero el silencio reza su canto gregoriano y pasional. (I, 861)

In Lorca's subsequent writings the theme takes on a host of different forms: unsatisfied adolescent longing ('la ilusión inquieta de un mañana imposible', *Libro de poemas*, I, 34); the poet's pre-occupation with the limitations of traditional poetic language ('Oh, qué dolor el tener / versos en la lejanía / de la pasión, y el cerebro / todo manchado de tinta', *Libro de poemas*, I, 99); the dramatist's awareness of the restrictions imposed on him by the conventions of the established theatre ('Yo y mi compañía venimos del teatro de los burgueses [...]. Yo y mi compañía estábamos encerrados. No os podéis imaginar qué pena teníamos', *Los títeres de cachiporra*. II, 61–2); the oppression of gypsies by dark forces: *pena negra*, civil guard, death... (*Romancero gitano*); the crushing of children, negroes and the poet himself by the impersonal machine civilisation of New York (*Poeta en Nueva York*)...

Vitality in La casa de Bernarda Alba

In Lorca's plays vitality is represented principally by women: by the Novia in *Bodas de sangre* with her passion for Leonardo, by the heroine of *Yerma* with her longing for children and, in *La casa de Bernarda Alba*, principally by Adela with her desire for Pepe el Romano. In each case the main representative of vitality is young, physically strong and passionate, her passion being stimulated by certain elements around her, especially by pointers to male vitality. The plane of vitality, then, in fact comprises two distinct elements: inherent female passion and external stimulus to passion. In *Bodas de sangre* the duality is fairly simple: the Novia and Leonardo. In *Yerma* it is more complex, for the external stimuli are more varied: María, Víctor, the Vieja, the fertile countryside, the *romería*. In *La casa de Bernarda Alba* the duality is even more complex, both in the representation of inherent vitality and in the multiplicity of external stimuli.

Under the former heading, Adela is the most important character: 'la más joven de nosotras y [la que] tiene ilusión' (25), strong enough to bring a bucking horse to its knees with the strength of her little finger (87), consumed by passion and prepared to overleap both mother and convention in the search for satisfaction (44). But her sisters, too, long for greater freedom and Martirio at least is tormented by passions that are possibly as great as Adela's own. Adela's sisters, then, serve — to some extent at least — as further representatives of female vitality.

As for the multiplicity of external stimuli, this is far greater than one finds even in *Yerma*. Pepe el Romano is the most obvious incitement to passion and the one most relevant to Adela, but many other offstage males are referred to also, some of them merely recalled from the past, others actually present outside the walls of the house: the priest and the former sacristan with their powerful voices ('un cántaro de agua', 'como un lobo', 7), the deceased father who used to lift up the maid's skirts behind the stable door (8), the widower at the funeral service, apparently interested in one of the village women (11), the male mourners with their salacious stories (17–18), the men who took Paca la Roseta away to the olive grove (18–19), the 'nuevo médico' whose arrival seems to have raised Martirio's spirits (22), men loading wheat in the yard (23), Enrique Humanes, a former would-be suitor of Martirio (23)... Some of these (and we are still only part way through Act I) serve as elements of enticement to Bernarda's daughters; all serve as reminders to the audience of the male vitality that is manifestly absent from the whitewashed interior of Bernarda's house. Add to these La Poncia's account of her own courtship, and sundry references to passions and escapades in and around the village, and María Josefa's clamour for 'un varón para casarme y para tener alegría' (33), and the insistence on heat, and repeated evocations of the joy and vitality of the countryside... and one appreciates better both the situation of Bernarda's daughters and the way in which Lorca presents it: latent passions and longings stimulated by a series of carefully orchestrated external incitements.

Though the incitements are less complex in *Bodas de sangre* and *Yerma*, the relationship of the heroines to those incitements is basically the same. Their dilemma, too, is similar in that, like Bernarda's daughters, the Novia and Yerma both find themselves faced with some sort of restriction on their vitality. At this point, however, the three plays diverge, for the type of restriction is different in each case. Since this offers the key to a much noted and little explained difference between the three plays it merits attention.

Repression in La casa de Bernarda Alba

The most obvious element of repression is the repulsively authoritarian Bernarda herself, 'tirana de todos los que la rodean' (5), with five chains for her five daughters (56), resolved to command until her death 'en lo mío y en lo vuestro' (32). Since this is obvious it need not detain us. Somewhat less obvious is the fact that Bernarda does not operate in a vacuum. To a large extent she responds to pressures exerted on her by the rigidly hierarchical and conformist society in which she lives.

This is most evident in the emphasis on reputation and the need to defend it against prying eyes and malicious tongues. 'De todo tiene la culpa esta crítica que no nos deja vivir', says Amelia (22), to which Magdalena, a moment later, adds, 'Nos pudrimos por el qué dirán' (24). It is in this context that one has to consider Bernarda's repeated insistence on decency (5, 17, 31) — or at least 'buena fachada' (73) —, her anger at her daughters' raised voices over the missing photo of Pepe el Romano ('Estarán las vecinas con el oído pegado a los tabiques', 53), and her annoyance that Poncia, 'una extraña' despite thirty years working in the house, should have witnessed the affair (56). Significantly, she is concerned not that her crazy mother may throw herself into the well but that the neighbours may see her in her madness (16), and at the end of the play her emphasis is less on the loss of Adela than on the proclaimed preservation of the girl's virginity (91). In these things, as in her eagerness to discover failings in others (5–6) and to see offenders punished (65–6), Bernarda is an extreme example of the vicious village 'crítica' and 'qué dirán' to which Amelia and Magdalena attribute their misfortunes. But the daughters themselves are not entirely dissimilar, and Magdalena, the most sympathetic of the five, is nevertheless quick to put a stop to Adela's outburst when the maid comes in, rebuking her with the words 'Ha estado a punto de oírte la criada' (29). In this as in other things Bernarda is not the only oppressor in the house. In their keenness to obviate village gossip and their general lack of charity towards one another the sisters uphold the very 'crítica' that they also decry, even Adela who informs Bernarda, '*Con retintín*', that Angustias has been spying on the men outside (17).[4] Similarly Poncia, with her desire not to 'manchar[se] de vieja' (44; cf. 'para que las gentes no escupan

[4] In this respect I find excessive polarisation in certain studies between characters who represent social conformity and those who oppose it. See especially Enrique Miralles, 'Concentración dramática en el teatro de Lorca', in *Archivum* (Oviedo) 21 (1971), 77–94, where all the sisters are grouped together as 'inconformistas'.

al pasar por esta puerta', 43). Finally, in this 'maldito pueblo sin río, pueblo de pozos, donde siempre se bebe el agua con el miedo de que esté envenenada' (14), Bernarda's most effective weapon against Poncia is her knowledge of the mother's dissolute life (59) and her greatest hold over Adelaida is her awareness of the parents' matrimonial complication (22). It matters little that Poncia and Adelaida were not responsible for their parents' actions. Uncharitable village morality is inclined to see them as inevitably sullied.

Closely related to the emphasis on public reputation is Bernarda's class snobbery: on the one hand, her statement that the poor are like animals, 'como si estuvieran hechos de otras sustancias' (9); on the other hand, her insistent references to what is appropriate to her own class ('Eso tiene la gente que nace con posibles', 15; '¿Es decente que una mujer de tu clase [...] ? ', 17). From the point of view of her daughters one aspect of this snobbery is especially important: her unwillingness to allow them to marry beneath them, as in her dismissal of Enrique Humanes ('¡Mi sangre no se junta con la de los Humanes mientras yo viva! Su padre fue gañán', 58) and in the following more general statement of her views: 'No hay en cien leguas a la redonda quien se pueda acercar a ellas. Los hombres de aquí no son de su clase. ¿Es que quieres que las entregue a cualquier gañán? ' (20). This, too, is an important element of repression on the Alba daughters.

Moreover, social position imposes with special rigour an accepted notion of the role of women, and Bernarda's 'Eso tiene ser mujer' (15) runs like a leitmotiv through the play. 'Hilo y aguja para las hembras. Látigo y mula para el varón. Eso tiene la gente que nace con posibles' (15). ' ¡Ay, quién pudiera salir también a los campos! ', exclaims Adela when the men are heard outside returning to the fields. ' ¡Cada clase tiene que hacer lo suyo! ', retorts Magdalena, and Martirio and Amelia agree (47). It is another reminder that Bernarda is not the only channel of repression in the Alba household. Whereas men are allowed both physical and moral freedom ('Se les perdona todo', 47), women are confined to the home. It is something that still exists in much of Andalusia, and in *La casa de Bernarda Alba* the situation is made worse by Bernarda's snobbery and her denial even of female company for her daughters. Nor are the daughters convinced that marriage would change anything fundamental, for it seems to mark simply a passage from parental

abuse to marital abuse, as with Adelaida who is now not allowed to
go out even to attend a neighbour's funeral (22). If one is a strong
character like Bernarda or Poncia one may make oneself the mistress
of one's domain ('Buen descanso ganó su pobre marido', 5; 'por
poco le dejo tuerto', 39), but one has little control over a husband's
extra-marital activities, whether these be sexual adventures with a
maid (8) or drinking in the local tavern (39), and it is Bernarda
herself who advises Angustias not to probe Pepe's 'preocupaciones':
'No le debes preguntar. Y cuando te cases, menos. Habla si él habla
y míralo cuando te mire. Así no tendrás disgustos' (74). Besides,
given the formality of courtship and the need for socially-based
parental approval there is little chance of marriage for love. What
men are mainly interested in is the dowry: 'la tierra, las yuntas y una
perra sumisa que les dé de comer' (23). 'Malditas sean las mujeres',
exclaims Magdalena (15) and Amelia apparently agrees: 'nacer mujer
es el mayor castigo' (48). Significantly, the subtitle of the play is
'drama de mujeres en los pueblos de España'.

The repression caused by the exaggerated acceptance of established customs and conventions is reinforced by Bernarda's procla-
mation of rigorous mourning for the dead father: to last for eight
years (at a time when five years was traditionally expected for a
deceased parent), with correspondingly extreme demands about the
form that it should take (14). Angustias suffers the consequences
when she is rebuked for going off to watch the men in the yard 'el
día de la misa de su padre' (17) and when Bernarda angrily removes
her face powder (31). But here as elsewhere it is Adela, the most
vital of the daughters, who suffers most. First it is the flowered fan
('¿Es éste el abanico que se da a una viuda? ', 14); then the green
dress that she was hoping to wear on her birthday (25) and for the
outing to the waterwheel (27). 'Lo que puedes hacer es teñirlo de
negro', says Martirio with characteristic nastiness (28), which reminds
us yet again that the sisters act as one another's jailers. 'Pienso que
este luto me ha cogido en la peor época de mi vida para pasarlo',
laments Adela when she hears of Pepe's proposed marriage to
Angustias (29). But she will not submit:

> (*Rompiendo a llorar con ira*.)
> ¡No, no me acostumbraré! Yo no quiero estar encerrada. No
> quiero que se me pongan las carnes como a vosotras. ¡No
> quiero perder mi blancura en estas habitaciones! ¡Mañana me

pondré mi vestido verde y me echaré a pasear por la calle! ¡Yo quiero salir! (29)

A moment later the cry is taken up by Angustias ('Madre, déjeme usted salir', 31) and shortly afterwards by the crazed María Josefa who expresses freely the longings that her five granddaughters are generally compelled to suppress (' ¡Déjame salir, Bernarda! [...]. ¡Quiero irme de aquí! ¡Bernarda! ¡A casarme a la orilla del mar, a la orilla del mar! *Telón rápido*', 33).

The main elements of repression in *La casa de Bernarda Alba*, then, are village gossip, class snobbery, the role of women in society, male attitudes, over-restrictive morality and customs — appropriately backed up by 'la ley de Dios' (43) — and, most immediately, the exaggerated acceptance of all these things by Bernarda and, though reluctantly, by most of her household. This is very different from what one finds in *Bodas de sangre* (1933) and *Yerma* (1934), and the importance of the difference justifies a detour. I confine myself to comparisons with *Bodas de sangre*.

The Different Repression in Bodas de sangre

In *Bodas de sangre* the vitality that seeks expression is basically that of the Novia. In the same way that Adela's longing finds response and enticement in Pepe el Romano, the Novia's finds response and enticement in Leonardo. But Leonardo is married and the Novia, with her sense of honour and her wounded pride at Leonardo's earlier abandonment of her, seeks refuge from her longing by marrying the Novio: 'Pero yo tengo orgullo. Por eso me caso. Y me encerraré con mi marido, a quien tengo que querer por encima de todo' (II, 607). This introduces a third element to reinforce the sense of honour and wounded pride: will power. These, then, are the three most immediately obvious elements of repression operating on the Novia's passion and, unlike those in *La casa de Bernarda Alba*, they are all internal. Of course, one can assume that society would share the Novia's view of the sanctity of marriage and applaud her self-imposed repression, but this is nowhere emphasised and, indeed, is scarcely mentioned. Nor is there any evidence of parental pressure on her in her decision to marry the Novio. Lorca's emphasis throughout is on internal pressures. Even honour, in so far as it appears in

Bodas de sangre, is internal honour (self esteem) rather than external honour (public reputation), and when the Novia finally yields to her passion and flees with Leonardo, it is despite herself, as though dragged along by an irresistible force ('porque me arrastras y voy, / y me dices que me vuelva / y te sigo por el aire / como una brizna de hierba', II, 649). Adela is very different. Though she feels similarly irresistible passion (64), internal restraints have little hold over her (' ¡Mi cuerpo será de quien yo quiera! ', 42), her main concern being with restraints imposed from outside – by Bernarda ('por encima de mi madre saltaría', 44), by others in the household ('Te he tenido miedo. ¡Pero ya soy más fuerte que tú! ', 44) and by the village beyond ('Todo el pueblo contra mí, quemándome con sus dedos de lumbre', 87). Consequently, in the breakaway towards the end of Act III she is not merely a slave of passion as the Novia is, but its defiant champion. With the breaking of her mother's stick it is as though external restraints themselves are broken. In an expression-istic television production the *muros gruesos* themselves might tremble.

   Bodas de sangre, then, differs from *La casa de Bernarda Alba* by its emphasis on internal rather than external restraints. But in *Bodas de sangre* there is something even deeper than internal restraints. To demonstrate this I need to summarise briefly points that I have made elsewhere about the structure of the play (MUP edition, 1980). Central to that structure is a triangle formed by the Novio, Leonardo and the Novia. Each point of the triangle is presented in turn – Novio (I, i), Leonardo (I, ii), Novia (I, iii) – with sundry satellite characters who are named by their relationship to one or other of the above three characters (e.g. I, i: the Novio's Madre, Vecina, and deceased father and brother). At the end of Act I the three points of the triangle come dangerously close together: the Novio has just left after his visit to the Novia, and Leonardo gallops by. But it is not simply three characters who come close together at the end of Act I; principally because of their deceased relatives and what has been said about them it is also three ominously complementary inheritances: the Novio's inheritance of violent death, Leonardo's inheritance of violent killing and the Novia's inheritance of no love for her husband. As the play proceeds, the evidence becomes stronger and the three points in the triangle are gradually drawn together. It is as though, through those complementary inheritances, fate itself guides the outcome. The Madre senses this even in the first scene of the play and epitomises her awareness by crossing herself in the last moment of the scene. She refers to the fatal plan more precisely at the end of Act II, when Leonardo and the Novia have run away together. Songs, too, point to underlying fatal forces and in the final act the Fates take on overtly physical form, as a succession of stylised figures: Woodcutters, Moon, Beggar Death and Spinning Girls. Passion has provided the impulse to action, circumstances have offered the means, and heredity, the most mysterious of the three, has guided the outcome. But behind all these things, one feels, was fate itself, the ultimate ruler and represser. More specific elements of repression are mere instruments, like the knife, *'para que* un día señalado entre las dos y las tres, / con este cuchillo / se queden dos hombres duros / con los labios amarillos' (II, 663; my italics). The inevitability of it all, and the final resignation in the Cross, prevents any questioning of the justice or injustice of the outcome.

In *La casa de Bernarda Alba* the situation is very different. Though there are references to parent–child similarities, they are more incidental than in *Bodas de sangre* ('[Angustias] que como su padre habla con la nariz', 27; cf. also 'Esa sale a sus tías', 20) or refer to minor characters ('Y [Adelaida] tiene el mismo sino de su madre y de su abuela', 23), and the spectator is encouraged to view them more realistically, with greater detachment, as elements of village life, even of village obscurantism. Certainly he has no feeling that they come together to complement one another in a plot-guiding fatal plan akin to that in *Bodas de sangre*. The only significant ancestor–child similarity in *La casa de Bernarda Alba* is one of vitality rather than repression: that of physical strength which runs from Bernarda's grandmother (16), through María Josefa (16), apparently through Bernarda herself, and on to Adela (87).

The Social Dimension in La casa de Bernarda Alba

The forces of repression in *Bodas de sangre*, then, are internal and controlled ultimately by fate; those in *La casa de Bernarda Alba* are external and man-made. The titles of the plays offer their own evidence: on the one hand, the imposition of blood (the ultimate bearer of fate for Lorca); on the other hand, the imposition of the man-made house. To understand the significance of this, we must probe our own experience. We live in an age of protest — protest against unemployment, against social conditions, against the despoiling of the environment, against allegedly inadequate financial rewards —, but where are the protests against fate or against natural death? Individuals may clamour against the inevitable, but protest is reserved for what can conceivably be changed. In *Bodas de sangre* Lorca offers no possibility of change. Everything is decreed. There is nothing the audience can do but lament, as in Greek tragedy. In *La casa de Bernarda Alba*, on the other hand, where the forces of repression are external and the final outcome is shown to be the consequence not of fate but of human failings — prejudice, parental oppression, inquisitorial imposition — we are encouraged not merely to lament but also to protest. Add to this the fact that *Yerma* presents an intermediate situation, and it seems that Lorca, in his final years — and he was still only in his thirties —, was evolving from being a dramatist of fate to being a dramatist of social concerns and even of social protest.[5]

Two further differences between the plays point in the same direction. In the first place, the Novia's dilemma, the choice between revolt (vitality) and conformity (repression), is associated, as in almost all Lorca's plays, with the presence of contrasting males: on the one hand, Leonardo, the dynamic male who offers an adequate response to the Novia's longing ('un río oscuro, lleno de ramas, que acercaba a mí el rumor de sus juncos y su cantar entre dientes', II, 660); on the other hand, the Novio, the inadequate male who is incapable of arousing or satisfying her passion ('un niñito de agua

---

[5] In saying this I am in disagreement with two mutually opposing lines of Lorcan criticism: on the one hand, with critics who, like Cedric Busette, emphasise the special importance of fate in all three plays ('el destino como un elemento todopoderoso y omnipresente', *11*, 26); on the other hand, with critics who, like José Monléon, emphasise the special importance of social repression in all three plays ('el enfrentamiento de la naturaleza con la represión social', *García Lorca, vida y obra de un poeta*, Aymá, Barcelona 1974, p. 65). In both cases the error (as I believe) arises from a failure to identify clearly the elements involved in the conflict. One finds something similar in those critics who refer to Lorca's increasing social awareness but fail to demonstrate it by reference to the obviously different elements of repression.

fría', II, 660). But apart from this innate inadequacy the Novio is blameless. So are Leonardo's wife and child. Consequently, however much we may sympathise with the Novia in her desire for self-fulfilment, we see also the undeserved consequences for others and are therefore not unreservedly on the side of revolt. Our sympathies are divided. Whether the Novia runs away with Leonardo or whether she remains with the Novio, the outcome will be unsatisfactory. The situation presented allows of no happy solution. As the audience we simply behold the conflict, share the torment and suffer the pathos. In *La casa de Bernarda Alba* it is very different. There is no suffering inadequate male and no abandoned wife and child. We are therefore more inclined to take the side of revolt. We do not feel that Adela and Pepe el Romano are as completely and justifiably tied as the Novia and Leonardo in *Bodas de sangre*.

This tendency on our part to side with revolt in *La casa de Bernarda Alba* is strengthened by a second relevant difference: the real-life unpleasantness of the elements of repression in the later play: the grotesquely domineering mother, the increasingly bitter and uncharitable family group, and, beyond this, the wider social group of the village, inquisitorial (as in the scene of the litany for the dead husband) and persecuting (as in the treatment of La Librada's daughter). These are things that arouse our anger and, therefore also, our sympathy for those who suffer from them. Whereas in *Bodas de sangre* we hesitated to take sides, in *La casa de Bernarda Alba* we want the heroine to revolt.

Moreover, in wanting Adela to revolt, we want others to revolt, too, for both she and the forces that repress her are shown to have wider relevance. On the one hand, her vitality has at its centre the 'pasiones admirables' (I, 859) that Lorca associated with young people, especially young women; on the other hand, the elements of repression are shown to apply also to others: to her sisters, to other women in the village (especially Adelaida and La Librada's daughter) and, still more widely, to women in general ('Eso tiene ser mujer', 'Nacer mujer es el mayor castigo'). Consequently, our sympathy and anger, too, take on a wider significance. As the subtitle of the play suggests, *La casa de Bernarda Alba* has a social dimension that in *Bodas de sangre* was almost entirely lacking.

The above internal evidence of Lorca's increasing social concerns is supported by external evidence, especially that of interviews. In

1934 Lorca declared his wish to 'llevar al teatro temas y problemas
que la gente tiene miedo de abordar', though at that point, it seems,
he was thinking of a 'tema moral' (II, 1036). The following year
he declared that 'el impulso de uno sería gritar todos los días al
despertar en un mundo lleno de injusticias y miserias de todo orden:
¡Protesto! ¡Protesto! ¡Protesto!' and referred to his plans for
'varios dramas de tipo humano y social' with different subject
matter from that of *Yerma* and *Bodas de sangre* (II, 1041–2). He also
referred, in the same interview, to an intended anti-war drama and,
in another interview of the same year, to a 'tragedia política' that
he was writing (II, 1062). Finally, in interviews given shortly before
his death he lamented 'el hambre que asola a los pueblos', alluded
to a 'problema religioso y económico-social' that he was currently
dealing with in a play (II, 1079), urged the need to 'meterse en el
fango hasta la cintura para ayudar a los que buscan las azucenas'
(II, 1083), and referred to 'un drama social, aún sin título' that he
had just completed (II, 1090). From accompanying references and
descriptions it seems unlikely that any of the above refers specifi-
cally to *La casa de Bernarda Alba*. The interviews do, however,
suggest, as the known plays themselves suggest, that Lorca was
becoming progressively more aware of social problems and more
concerned to incorporate them into his theatre.

And yet, despite all this, it is doubtful whether *La casa de
Bernarda Alba* can properly be described as a work of social protest.
As a starting-point one can take the Criada's outcry against the
wealth of the house where she works and the contrasting reference
to her own mud hovel (8). It reveals class consciousness and emphasises inequality and exploitation, and the point is further strengthened by her reference to the forced attentions of the master of the
house. If the play had continued in the same vein it could reasonably
have been described as a work of social criticism and even of social
protest. But it does not. The main emphasis of the play is not on
the exploitation of the poor by the rich but on the problems of
women born into a repressively conservative and hierarchical rural
family of considerable wealth and social standing. Economic con-
siderations are important, as one sees from the contrast between
Angustias's situation as the principal inheritor of her father's wealth
and that of her four sisters, with 'pan y uvas por toda herencia' (6).
But this inheritance of 'pan y uvas' is still considerable and the

family has 'la mejor manada de estos contornos' (69). In the words of the class-conscious Criada, '¡Ya quisiera tener yo lo que ellas!' (6).

Misfortunes, then, do not arise primarily from economic and social deprivation, nor from any form of class conflict. Consequently, Isaac Rubio's statement, 'La posesión de la riqueza determina la división neta entre las clases' (29, 173), though true, is only marginally relevant to the main action of the play. Nor can the 'ausencia de conciencia de clase' that Poncia reveals in such statements as 'Yo tengo la escuela de tu madre' (39) and 'No vayas contra la ley de Dios' (43) be dismissed as mere 'penuria ideólogica' (29, 176). The morality that Bernarda upholds as specially relevant to her own class is also, basically, that of the village as a whole, as one sees from sundry references by the daughters ('De todo tiene la culpa esta crítica que no nos deja vivir', 22), from Adelaida's fear that her parents' matrimonial complication may become public knowledge (22) and from the villagers' treatment of La Librada's daughter (65). Even Bernarda, with her ever-present desire to declare her neighbours' failings, admits that Paca la Roseta 'es la única mujer mala que tenemos en el pueblo' and Poncia adds 'Porque no es de aquí. Es de muy lejos' (19). The overall impression, then, despite the Criada's outburst at the beginning, is not of class divisions and economic deprivation but of narrow, inquisitorial mean-mindedness in a rigidly traditionalist village society.

This, of course, is a moral problem as much as a social problem and, despite my earlier emphasis on external repression in *La casa de Bernarda Alba*, it is not the sort of problem that allows of easy solution or, in consequence, invites specific protest. This is especially true of the privileged position of men and their selfishly repressive attitude to women. It is a question of people's whole psychological outlook, especially since women themselves accept the injustice, even strong characters like Bernarda (74) and Poncia (39). Even the most relevant economic factor in the play, that of Angustias's privileged position, is less important in itself than as a pointer to Pepe's response and thus to male attitudes, and these are significantly emphasised elsewhere also, with reference to Enrique Humanes: '¡Qué les importa a ellos la fealdad! A ellos les importa la tierra, las yuntas y una perra sumisa que les dé de comer' (23).

But in *La casa de Bernarda Alba* there is something even more important than male attitudes — or the general panorama of repression of which they form part. The following exchange will serve to illustrate the point:

PONCIA.   Hace años vino otra de éstas y yo misma di dinero a mi
     hijo mayor para que fuera. Los hombres necesitan estas cosas.
ADELA.   Se les perdona todo.
AMELIA.   Nacer mujer es el mayor castigo.
MAGDALENA.   Y ni nuestros ojos siquiera nos pertenecen.

(Se oye un cantar lejano que se va acercando.)   (47–8)

The extract starts with evidence of Poncia's indulgent attitude to men's sexual adventures — first in a specific case ('mi hijo mayor'), then with characteristic generalisation ('los hombres') — and the indulgence is emphasised by contrast with her restrictive attitude to women of a few moments before (43–4). Adela and Amelia draw the general inferences that the audience itself is encouraged to make: first the privileged position of men; then the deprived position of women. In view of interpretations of the play in terms of class conflict it is important to note, in passing, that there is no suggestion of class disagreement on this: a servant makes the initial point and two daughters of the household develop it. In so far as inequality is dramatically relevant it is sexual rather than social inequality. But even sexual inequality is of relatively little importance in itself. In the juxtaposition of male freedom ('Se les perdona todo') and female repression ('Nacer mujer es el mayor castigo') the progression is significantly from the former to the latter and it is here that Lorca's greater emphasis lies (cf. the play's subtitle). Male freedom, then, serves principally as a foil to bring out women's subjection, and male attitudes increase the subjection. Moreover, Lorca is not concerned with mere generic 'women', but with real-life persons in a specific situation. The point is clearly illustrated in the next words in the above passage: Magdalena's 'Y ni nuestros ojos siquiera nos pertenecen'. On one level they can be seen as a continuation of Amelia's preceding generalisation: that is, as an image of women's deprivation, since even their eyes do not belong to them. But in a house where peeping out of windows is a half-forbidden life-line, they also have special relevance to the Alba sisters and therefore mark a transition back from generalisation to their own specific situation. In case there should be any doubt about this, the point is emphasised by the immediately following stage direction with its indication of the offstage presence of the reapers and, a few moments later, by the most rebellious daughter's 'Vamos a verlos por la ventana de mi cuarto'. Lorca, then, having started from the specific, with Poncia's 'mi hijo', has passed via generalisation to remind us of the wider implications, and has returned finally to the specific situation of the Alba daughters. It illustrates admirably Lorca's view of the theatre as 'una tribuna libre donde los hombres pueden poner en evidencia morales viejas o equívocas y explicar con *ejemplos vivos normas eternas* del corazón y del sentimiento del hombre' (my italics).[6] It is also a superbly written passage, apparently simple but with all the skill and sophistication that one is inclined to associate with his more obviously poetic tragedies, *Bodas de sangre* and *Yerma*.

This brings me to Lorca's ultimate aim, beyond even the interplay of vitality and repression in the Bernarda Alba household: the adequate expression of the resulting conflict in dramatic form. It is with this that I am principally concerned in the rest of my Introduction.

REALISM AND POETRY

The question of realism and poetry in *La casa de Bernarda Alba* has concerned critics more than any other. Is the play a notable 'realistic drama' (*22*, 7) or is it 'a highly poetic drama' (*23*, 470), even 'una obra tan poética como las otras del autor' (*24*, 135)?

Lorca's own statements on the subject are a useful starting-point. In a one-sentence preface to the play he warns us that 'estos tres actos tienen la intención de un documental fotográfico' and, according to the critic Adolfo Salazar who lived close by at the time the play was written, 'cada vez que [Lorca] terminaba una escena venía corriendo, inflamado de entusiasmo. "¡Ni una gota de poesía! — exclamaba —. ¡Realidad! ¡Realismo puro!"' (cited in *34*, 37–8). Morla Lynch, too, who was present at the June reading of the play, refers in his diary to the play's 'impresionante realismo', 'penoso naturalismo' and 'pavoroso realismo' (*op. cit.*, pp. 484, 488), and

---

[6] Cited by Antonio Buero Vallejo, *Tres maestros ante el público*, Alianza, Madrid 1973, p. 154.

Lorca himself, through his comments, may well have prompted the expressions. But all such statements have to be seen in context. Lorca had been criticised by some for excessive lyricism in his earlier plays. Though he tended to dismiss his critics as 'putrefactos', he was sensitive to adverse comments and may well have been keen to emphasise — and even overemphasise — the greater realism of his latest play.[7] As for the words '¡Ni una gota de poesía! ', they can of course be taken seriously, as an indication of the author's belief that the poetry has now been completely integrated into the action, leaving no 'drops' on the surface. But they are worthy of a prologue to one of his farces and can also be seen as a deflating knock at his critics. In any case, Lorca himself showed that he did not reject the poet's function. In April 1936, when *La casa de Bernarda Alba* was presumably well advanced, even if it was not yet committed to paper, he defined theatre as 'la poesía que se levanta del libro y se hace humana' (II, 1078) and in the one-sentence preface to the play it is significantly the 'poeta' who informs us of its documentary intentions. This brings us back to the central problem: realism or poetry?

It also brings us face to face with two of the most important and elastic terms in literary criticism and obliges me to indicate the way in which I use them. Literary creation involves three elements: the writer (as both personality and artist), the world around him (objective reality) and language (the means by which some form of reconciliation between the former two can be communicated to others).[8] Realism, in the sense in which I here use the term, implies emphasis on objective reality rather than on the writer's inner world and the use of language to communicate reality — or at least a semblance of reality — free from distortion by the writer's vision. Poetry, on the other hand, involves the active participation of

[7] One finds something similar in his reaction to *Romancero gitano*-prompted suggestions that he was a gypsy poet and in his emphasis on a change of direction (II, 1231–2).

[8] Here and in what follows I use 'language' in a broad sense, to include also non-linguistic language appropriate to the theatre: decor, dress, movements and gestures, sounds and silence, colours, etc. It is the point at which literature joins hand with other arts (painting, mime, music...) and incorporates means of communication appropriate to those other arts.

the writer's inner being at the expense of the world around him, with interpretation, selection, moulding and ultimately recreation of that world by means of language. Realism and poetry complement one another, then: at one end of the literary spectrum lies realism; at the other end, poetry; between the two, various mixtures. But neither realism nor poetry can exist in a pure form: realism, because it cannot completely escape the shaping spirit of the writer; poetry, because it cannot totally dispense with surrounding reality. As a critic one is therefore concerned with different degrees of realism and poetry in different works, and the words 'realism' and 'poetry' are most commonly used to indicate different approximations, often with some form of qualification to indicate the particular type of approximation. Thus, Realism (with a capital R) serves to indicate a type of approximation to reality that one associates especially with literature of the second half of the nineteenth century, and *neorrealismo* to indicate a new type of approximation characteristic of the 1950s in Spain. Similarly, the word 'poetry' in 'Spanish poetry since 1870' refers to a literary genre that is commonly (though by no means always) more poetic than others, and *poesía pura* to a type of poetry that is notable for the poet's aspiration to raise up both self and reader from crude real-life involvement.

This is all rather sweeping and over-simplified. A philosopher might reject my notion of objective reality on the grounds that no known reality exists independently of man's perception of it, and certain critics would argue that the poet's inner reality, being a reality, should also be incorporated into the term 'realism'. In both cases, then, criticism would be aimed at the distinction that I establish between what is within the writer and what is around him. They are points of view that the reader should bear in mind. I maintain my distinction because of its usefulness — realism that includes virtually everything indicates nothing — and because my own use of the word 'realism' keeps me close to familiar, everyday uses of that and related words ('real', 'reality', etc.). Similarly, I find that students are helped through many problems by emphasis on the fact that poetry is characterised especially by the importance given to the shaping inner spirit at the expense of the world around and by the consequent special demands on language, through which surrounding reality must be transformed. Poetic language is then seen in its proper perspective: not as mere adornment (the 'cake and icing' view of literature) but as a necessary means of transformation and communication, inseparable from what is communicated.[9]

In view of this, the guiding questions throughout the present section are: first, to what extent did Lorca subject himself to reality in *La casa de Bernarda Alba* and, conversely, to what extent did he subject reality to himself, either as a personality or as an artist; secondly, in so far as he subjected reality to himself, how did he use language to communicate his own particular view of reality. As with the conflict between vitality and repression, I find it helpful to break the problem down into a series of less complex component parts.

Fact and Fiction

In his book *En España con Federico García Lorca* Morla Lynch records the following reference by Lorca to the real-life basis of the play:

> Hay, no muy distante de Granada, una aldehuela en la que mis padres eran dueños de una propiedad pequeña: Valderrubio. En la casa vecina y colindante a la nuestra vivía "doña Bernarda", una viuda de muchos años que ejercía una inexorable y tiránica vigilancia sobre sus hijas solteras. Prisioneras privadas de todo albedrío, jamás hablé con ellas; pero las veía pasar como sombras, siempre silenciosas y siempre de negro vestidas. Ahora bien — prosigue —: había en el confín del patio un pozo medianero, sin agua, y a él descendía para espiar a esa familia extraña cuyas actitudes enigmáticas me intrigaban. Y pude observarla. Era un infierno mudo y frío en ese sol africano, sepultura de gente viva bajo la férula inflexible de cancerbero

---

[9] As an example of the 'cake and icing' approach I quote from a study published on *La casa de Bernarda Alba*: 'The author meant to depict the situation in a stark definitive manner (" [...] documental fotográfico") in order to impress his audience; at the same time, his conscience demanded that he impart an artistic touch to the scene.' For me — and presumably for most critics — the organising of material into an 'impressive' documentary is part of the poetic (or 'artistic') process. Poetry and artistry are not simply added in 'touches', at least not in a work of the quality of this play.

oscuro. Y así nació — termina diciendo — *La casa de Bernarda Alba*. (*op. cit.*, pp. 488–9)

From later evidence it seems that Lorca's dependence on reality was both greater and less than this: greater, because he drew more widely than he here indicated on real-life characters and incidents; less, because the widow's oppression of her daughters seems to have been less a reality than a Lorcan interpretation of reality. In the former respect one notes, for example, Francisco García Lorca's (hereafter FGL) and Antonio Ramos Espejo's (ARE) emphasis on the number of characters, both onstage and offstage, who actually existed: Bernarda Alba herself (Frasquita Alba in real life) and four daughters, Poncia ('pero no estaba de criada en casa de Frasquita, sino en otra', ARE, 62), María Josefa ('la abuela de unas amigas nuestras y lejanísimas parientes [...], víctima de una locura erótica', FGL, 377), Pepe el Romano (in real life, José Benavides, Pepico el de Roma, ARE, 62), the man (Prudencia's husband in the play) who refused to leave his house by the door, Prudencia herself, Enrique Humanes ...[10] On the other hand one notes the lack of serious evidence to support the view that the real-life Frasquita Alba was a tyrannical mother and one recalls Francisco García Lorca's observation that, though the characters in *La casa de Bernarda Alba* are taken from reality, 'ninguno es fiel a su remoto modelo, salvo en el detalle', and that the plot itself is 'enteramente inventada' (*loc. cit.*).

Lorca, then, drew extensively on real-life elements but adapted them to a plot of his own invention. By what process? We cannot be sure, but the available evidence justifies a hypothesis. Lorca, we know, tended to see the world in terms of vitality and repression and to emphasise this duality in his writings. If young monks or nuns amidst the 'paz y tranquilidad' of a monastery or convent could prompt in him reflections on the torment of repression, an

---

[10] Francisco García Lorca, *Federico y su mundo* (1980), 2nd. ed., Alianza, Madrid 1981, pp. 376–8; Antonio Ramos Espejo, 'En Valderrubio, Granada: La casa de Bernarda Alba', in *Triunfo*, February 1981, pp. 58–63. Cf. also: 'But not a single one of the characters, even those who do not take part but are merely alluded to, and not a single act of those who serve as background proceed directly from the poet's imagination' (Francisco García Lorca, Introduction to *Lorca, Three Tragedies* (1947), Penguin, p. 28).

Andalusian village household composed of a widow and four unmarried daughters, all in mourning, could presumably do the same.
It matters little whether the real-life widow was a tyrant or whether
the village atmosphere was in fact oppressive. To Lorca, with his
obsessive concern with the repression of vitality, they must almost
inevitably have seemed so, especially when recalled a quarter of a
century later. The similarity between what Lorca stated to Morla
Lynch and what he presents in his play may even confirm the
sincerity of his vision.

But it is less the vision that matters than the adequate communication of that vision to others. The principal means by which Lorca
does communicate will be considered in succeeding pages. But two
details are especially relevant to the present section. In order to
bring out the conflict between vitality and repression Lorca needed
not only to make Frasquita into a tyrannical Bernarda; he needed
also to emphasise the vitality of the daughters. He could have done
this by vitalising one or more of the four real-life daughters but
chose to add an extremely passionate fifth daughter, Adela, 'enteramente creación del poeta', except for the name, 'que procede de
una realidad circundante' (FGL, 377), and for the odd detail apparently taken from one of Lorca's cousins (ARE, 60). Also, to
give expression to the daughters' suppressed desires and threatening
revolt, Lorca the artist needed María Josefa and here recalled another
fragment of reality: a crazy old woman whom he had known as a
child, but in a completely different, urban environment (FGL, 377).

This is all very different from the impression given, for example,
by Schonberg and Auclair, with their emphasis on the well episode
(above, xxxii).[11] This was clearly a recollection from childhood
('desde el plano de la niñez', FGL, 376) and in 1936 Lorca supposed
that the real-life women were perhaps all dead (Morla, 489). Schonberg's emphasis on the hours that Lorca must have spent in the well,
observing, and Auclair's placing of the episode in 1935 both overemphasise a realist approach at the expense of a poetic one. But
Lorca's merit lay not in prolonged observation and documentation
within a specific area of reality, but in the skilful incorporation

---

[11] Jean-Louis Schonberg, *Federico García Lorca*, Plon, Paris 1956,
pp. 314–19; Marcelle Auclair, *Enfances et mort de García Lorca*,
Editions du Seuil, Paris 1968, pp. 334–8.

of disparate real-life fragments into a wholly personal, integrated and effective work of art.

This carries us beyond the question of fact and fiction — initially to the problem of verisimilitude.

Verisimilitude: (1) Situations and Context

Realism, I have said, implies emphasis on objective reality and the use of language to communicate reality — or at least a semblance of reality — free from distortion by the writer's personal vision. The previous section, especially with the transition indicated in my final sentence, marks a shift from reality itself to a semblance of reality and it is this with which we are most commonly concerned when we refer to realism in literature. Here the guiding criterion is not so much whether characters and plot were taken from reality as whether they are true to life: that is, whether characters appear as real-life persons who respond convincingly to real-life situations in a real-life context. In the present section I shall consider situations and context; in the following section I shall consider characters.

The basic situation presented in *La casa de Bernarda Alba* is that of a household of unmarried daughters oppressed by a tyrannical mother and, beyond and through her, by the over-restrictive morality, customs and conventions of the village in which they live. The liberated urban spectator of the twentieth century may have difficulty in accepting it as a real-life picture and several critics, keen to emphasise that the play is poetic rather than realistic, have doubted the general validity of Lorca's view:

> Y a continuación viene el subtítulo *Drama de mujeres en los pueblos de España* que parece indicar, con la generalización 'en los pueblos', algo sintomático y común a la vida pueblerina española. Sin embargo, un conocedor aun superficial de la vida de esos pueblos sabe que un caso, como el que en la obra se expone, sería imposible en la mayoría de los pueblos de la España vivida por el autor, y aceptable sólo como extraordinario y raro incluso en tierras andaluzas o acaso castellanas. (7, 387)

Though readily accepting that Bernarda's family offers an extreme case, I am myself unable to see it as 'una familia andaluza "*al margen*"' (21, 91). Apart from Lorca's repeated generalisations from

the particular (as in 'Eso tiene ser mujer') my own contact with
specific Andalusian villages and the situation of young women
in those villages convinces me that Lorca was presenting a real-life
problem of more than marginal relevance. Little or no communication with the world outside, little contact with potential marriage
partners, the excessive dependence on gossip brought by the maid,
the excited waiting for the annual *romería*, the illusion of a visit by
or to a relation living in another village − or perhaps even a town −,
the excitement caused by the arrival of a travelling vendor of laces
or pots and pans, and frequently, in this society where a woman's
proper role is seen to lie in marriage and motherhood, the fear,
evolving gradually to resigned despair, that one may finish up as an
abandoned spinster or, at best, married to someone for whom one
has neither love nor respect... all this I see − and have seen − as
reality. I find reality, too, in Lorca's contrasting emphasis on the
greater freedom and sexual liberties of men, as also in his emphasis
on social stratification, even within extremely small villages where
a more romantic notion might suggest a democratic sense of harmony and togetherness. The problems and tensions of modern
village co-operatives, one feels, would have caused Lorca no surprise
at all.

But it is not only real-life situations, problems and tensions that
one finds in *La casa de Bernarda Alba*. The whole setting of the play
is specific and down-to-earth: the house itself, the tolling funeral
bells, Poncia who comes in eating bread and chorizo, the maid
making everything spotless for the expected funeral guests and
wondering if there are enough chairs, the beggar woman and her
child ... The conversations, too: the maids who grumble about
Bernarda behind her back and Bernarda who rebukes the maids to
their faces, references to the heat and to progress with the harvest,
village gossip, earthy anecdotes from the maid, traditional greetings,
blessings and curses, colloquial expressions that one immediately
associates with Spanish village life... One finds something similar in
Bodas de sangre, most notably in Act I, Scene iii, but in *La casa de
Bernarda Alba* the same earthiness runs through the whole play.
There is no place here for stylised Woodcutters, Moon and Beggar
Death, or for the lyrical language with which they comment on
the action in *Bodas de sangre*. The impression given by *La casa
de Bernarda Alba* is that of a developing real-life situation in a

down-to-earth real-life context. Significantly, the most extraordinary events and situations in the play — the Paca la Roseta escapade, the mobbing of La Librada's daughter, Bernarda's shooting at Pepe and Adela's death — all occur offstage. Our concern as an audience is less with these things themselves than with the response to them of the characters who are actually onstage, within the narrow confines of a single village house. This brings us directly to the question of characterisation.

Verisimilitude: (2) Characters

In real life we tend to recognise people rather than know them. In this respect drama, with its special emphasis on physical appearance, dress, gestures, tone of voice, facial expressions, is potentially the most realistic of literary genres. But people are not mere physical appearance. Beneath the externals that we perceive are individual human characters, complex, difficult to understand, pushed and pulled in different directions by different impulses and motivations, and behind these impulses and motivations, prompting them or influencing them, is a complex network of pressures and prejudices: economic, social, political, national... These characters and pressures, too, are part of reality. Because of their complexity and because much of the complexity is internal (character) or insidious (pressures), drama, with its emphasis on perceived reality and its greater need for brevity and streamlining, is potentially less realistic than the novel. The questions one then has to ask oneself, in considering the problem of realism in a given play, is whether and to what extent, through perceived reality, that play conveys the impression of underlying complexity, both of characters and of pressures on characters. It is these questions that I wish to consider with reference to *La casa de Bernarda Alba*. Limitations of space oblige me to illustrate rather than survey comprehensively.

As a starting-point I quote the summary of my findings on the three characters who together constitute the central 'Triangle of Action' in *Bodas de sangre*:

> 'Una mujer quemada', 'un poquito de agua' and 'un río oscuro': a woman filled with longing, a man who is an inadequate response to that longing and a man of passion who is an adequate response. They are basic elements rather than

individuals, and the characteristics given to the three central
protagonists serve to emphasize their elemental function.
There is no individuality for the sake of individuality. *Bodas
de sangre* is a play of essential forces and essential relationships.
The very names of the characters are significant. (*op. cit.*, xxii)

It is not certain that all critics would accept this view without
reservations, and C.B. Morris has gone further than others in study-
ing the same three characters as complex, real-life individuals.[12]
Nevertheless, even when maximum allowance has been made for
Morris's evidence, I find nothing in the above that I should wish to
change. The real-life details that Morris points to all contribute, I
believe, to the elemental function of the characters concerned.
Everything in *Bodas de sangre* is subordinated to a streamlined
fatal plan.

This is less clearly the case in *La casa de Bernarda Alba*. In
the first place, since there is no fatal plan, the spectator's guiding
question is not so much 'How will it happen? ' as 'What will happen? '. This is important because it causes the spectator himself to
streamline less and to pay maximum attention to every clue, in the
realisation that an apparently incidental remark may point to subsequent plot development. But it is Lorca himself who principally
streamlines less. Whereas in *Bodas de sangre* one is encouraged to
consider almost exclusively the function of various characters, in
La casa de Bernarda Alba one is made more aware of characters
as individuals. Of course, Adela is still essentially the Lorcan woman
of vitality, young, strong and beautiful, and Pepe el Romano is still
the epitome of male enticement, young, macho and impatient of
social constraints, and in this I find them scarcely distinguishable
from the Novia and Leonardo. But the plane of male enticement is
not represented solely by Pepe el Romano and reference has already
been made to the profusion of offstage males who make their own
contribution. More importantly, the plane of female vitality is not
contained wholly within Adela. To some extent it is represented
also by her four sisters, each with her own individual responses to
Bernarda's oppression. But these four sisters cannot be said merely
to represent female vitality. As was shown in a previous section,

[12]*Bodas de sangre*. Critical Guides to Spanish Texts, 26 (London
1980), 30–9.

they also, in different ways and to differing degrees, accept and even uphold oppression. The conflicting forces in the play are therefore more fragmented than they were in *Bodas de sangre* and characters are more complex; consequently — since I take such fragmentation and complexity to be characteristic of real life — they are also more realistic. In this I find myself in disagreement with Torrente Ballester's view of the Alba sisters as mere 'abstracciones poéticas, seres convencionales y acaso simbólicos' (*3*, 114).

But one can go further than this and, as an example — to show that even vitality and repression do not explain everything in the sisters' characters — I take the most complex sister, Martirio. There is little I feel able to add to Seybolt's perceptive study (*30*) and much that I am obliged to omit. Martirio, like Adela, stands out from the remaining sisters by her great passions and longings; thence also, presumably, by her suffering from Bernarda's oppression. But whereas Adela reveals her revolt from the beginning (symbolically with the flowered fan and, more realistically, with her green dress and her 'Yo no quiero estar encerrada', 29) Martirio repeatedly indicates conformity and absence of passion: gives her mother a black fan (14), says she does not feel the heat (14), declares her fear of men and her acceptance of the fact that she will never marry (23), and expresses her joy at Angustias's forthcoming marriage (26). Initially we are inclined to accept this evidence at its face value, but Magdalena, the most balanced and humane of the sisters — and the one whose guidance to the spectator is most reliable —, puts it in a new light with the words ' ¡Nunca he podido resistir tu hipocresía! ' (27). Martirio, then, has perhaps been misleading us and concealing her real thoughts and passions. And of course this proves to be so. She too suffers from Bernarda's oppression and later turns angrily on her mother (54); she especially feels the heat (with its symbolic resonances) and longs for the cool of November (49–50); she too desires Pepe — as much as Adela does — and steals his photo and hides it between her bed sheets (54); and she is no more pleased than others about Angustias's forthcoming marriage and reminds her sister that she has won Pepe only because of her wealth (56).[13] This last point illustrates

[13] Significantly Poncia's only two errors of appreciation both concern Martirio: first, when she tells Adela that Martirio is the sister

(Continued overleaf)

another of Martirio's main characteristics: her envy and, beyond that, her viciousness at other people's happiness or good fortune. It first shows itself in Act I, when she greets Adela's illusion about her green dress – at a rare moment of harmony and laughter among the sisters – with the words 'Lo que puedes hacer es teñirlo de negro' (28), and it reappears on several occasions thereafter, down to the final moments of the play when it is Martirio's false report of Pepe's death that precipitates Adela's suicide. 'Esa es la peor', says Poncia with her usual perspicacity; 'Es un pozo de veneno. Ve que el Romano no es para ella y hundiría el mundo si estuviera en su mano' (81). A few moments later Martirio more or less confesses it herself (87). 'Abstracción poética'? 'Ser convencional'? Or a complex real-life character who makes the critic's generalisations about vitality and repression seem almost irrelevant?

This complexity in Lorca's treatment of Martirio arises, in part at least, from the nature of hypocrisy, with its divergence between inner being and outward expression. But it is not only in the treatment of Martirio that one finds complexity and ambivalence in *La casa de Bernarda Alba*. Bernarda, for example, has been variously seen to epitomise 'una filosofía y una tradición', that of the Calderonian code of honour (*1*, 46), a psychological flaw of 'acatamiento [to village morality] y voluntad de dominio' (*3*, 125) and, with expressed reservations about this last interpretation, a class-based weakness arising from her socio-economic position (*6*, 139–40). Since there is evidence to support all these views, one cannot identify Bernarda exclusively with any one of them. Here, too, the complexity is greater than in any of Lorca's earlier plays. But there is further evidence that adds to the complexity. Bernarda is less confident than her arrogance would suggest and her apparent persecution mania makes her susceptible to 'malos sueños' (60) and, thence also, a victim of the moral system that she herself especially upholds. Moreover, her mother is repeatedly associated with the sea

(Continued from page xxxix)

who loves her most (42) and, secondly, when, a few minutes later, she is 'extrañada' to find Pepe's photo in Martirio's bed (54). Even the audience's most trusted guide, it seems, here fails to realise how envy and repressed passions may distort normal relationships and behaviour patterns.

and it is there that she longs to go. The men here, she says, 'huyen de
las mujeres', 'yo me quiero ir a mi pueblo', '¡A casarme a la orilla del
mar!' (32–3). María Josefa, then, is from a village on the coast and
she carries in her blood the sexual vitality that Lorca associated with
the sea. Perhaps Bernarda too, since her father built the house where
they now live (56). Certainly she appears to have the physical strength
that was Lorca's principal pointer to sexual vitality and it is she who
curses this 'maldito pueblo sin río, pueblo de pozos' (14). Besides,
she has had two husbands and five daughters, and in a rare moment
of pathos when she is described as '*desolada*' and even refers to her
'desolación' she pulls herself together with the thought that the dis-
ciplining of her daughters is her 'obligación' (56). Is her rigorous
morality, then, that of an outsider anxious to be, as Spaniards say,
'más papista que el papa', with the consequent suppression and defor-
mation of her own inner being? [14] It does after all seem strange that
one so apparently rigorous in moral matters should have allowed the
daughter of a former prostitute to become her chief servant and that
she should encourage her to bring the sort of titillating accounts of
village immorality from which she seeks to isolate her daughters (18–
19). Her sadism is relevant too ('Es capaz de sentarse encima de tu
corazón y ver cómo te mueres durante un año sin que se le cierre
esa sonrise fría que lleva en su maldita cara', 5), especially the sexually sadistic treatment that she demands for La Librada's daughter.
Finally, two muttered insults of her by villagers, '¡Vieja lagarta
recocida!' and '¡Sarmentosa por calentura de varón!' (11), both of
which have sexual connotations, suggest that they at least see her
as sexually repressed. Since one of the speakers was the audience's
most trusted guide, La Poncia, perhaps we ourselves should accept
the suggestion. Of course we cannot be sure and this, too, is characteristic of the play – and of reality. In *Bodas de sangre*, with its
clearer guidance on less complex characters, we should have been
left in no doubt.

---

[14] Compare the Novia's mother in *Bodas de sangre*:
NOVIA.   Mi madre era de un sitio donde había muchos árboles. De
tierra rica.
CRIADA.   ¡Así era ella de alegre!
NOVIA.   Pero se consumió aquí. (II, 599)

I find complexity and ambivalence also in other characters but to a far less extent.[15] I also find realism in the fact that we cannot immediately distinguish between four of Bernarda's five daughters, especially since they are all dressed in black, and that we only come to know them after several readings or performances. Nevertheless, despite all the above, one must be wary of exaggerating Lorca's move to realism. In an earlier section I referred to the frequent references to offstage males (above, xvii). Some of these, I said, serve as enticements to Bernarda's daughters; all serve as reminders to the audience of the male vitality that is manifestly absent from the whitewashed interior of Bernarda's house. I see the distinction as important. If Lorca's main concern had been with psychological realism, he would presumably have integrated his many pointers to offstage male vitality more fully into the Alba daughter's experience and, at the same time, have encouraged a more detached view-point in his audience. But his aim, it seems, was not merely to study the impact of conflicting vitality and repression on his characters, but also, more importantly, to involve the audience itself directly in that conflict. I see this as an essentially poetic approach.

Moreover, despite the greater complexity of characters in *La casa de Bernarda Alba*, function is still of prime importance and no individual trait is allowed to detract from that function. Thus, Adela is above all the epitome of vitality that demands expression and her name is significant: she is 'la que se *adela*nta' (64), the one who has 'fuerza para *adela*ntar[se] (85), in contrast to Martirio ('Martirio: cara de martirio', 83), the epitome of repressed vitality and the clearest expression of Leonardo's — and Lorca's — notion that 'Callar y quemarse es el castigo más grande que nos podemos echar encima' (II, 607). Similarly: Pepe el Romano is the incarnation of male vitality, with a name that brings together both village immediacy (Pepe) and mythic stature (el Romano); Bernarda is above all the oppressor and, as her surname suggests, the arch whitewasher

[15] See, however, Medardo Fraile's view that 'La Poncia is, by far, the most mysterious and complex character in the play' (*13*, 12–13), a view that is strengthened by Spires' emphasis on La Poncia's hypocrisy, self-contradiction, insinuations and 'game of dual intent', all part, he believes, of her 'program of insidious revenge' against Bernarda (*22*).

of events (*albo, white*; cf. 'Tú empieza a blanquear el patio', 21, with associated emphasis on cleanliness); María Josefa is a means of exteriorising the daughters' suppressed longings and of essentialising the conflict (with a name that, in view of the lamb and nativity references, may reasonably recall Mary and Joseph and therefore offer a further contrast to Bernarda, the cruel parent who denies life, despite the ironic 'dawn' that is also suggested by her name); Poncia is the classical Lorcan peasant woman who best understands what is really going on and therefore acts as a chorus-like guide to the audience ...[16] Perhaps only the Criada's class-based outburst near the beginning of Act I (8) and Prudencia's presence at the beginning of Act III are notably less relevant to the main, streamlined thrust of the play than is usual in Lorca.

Streamlining and Significance

The points made in the last two paragraphs suggest a departure from mere realism. So does the evidence of streamlining that was offered earlier under 'Vitality and Repression'. Reality in *La casa de Bernarda Alba* has been selected and concentrated around a central theme and thereby been made to serve the communication of that theme. Moreover, because of the repeated oscillations between the particular and the general (cf. above, xxviii) we are persuaded that, in their

[16] It is not impossible that Poncia's name, too, is significant, for it is the feminine form of Pontius and, after fruitless attempts to warn Bernarda of the dangers, she does finally, though only at the very end, wash her hands of the situation: 'Yo no puedo hacer nada. Quise atajar las cosas, pero ya me asustan demasiado' (80; *7*, 388). Her name has been related also to its etymology ('the bridge', *13*, 15). Comparable relevance — though not always the same relevance — has been suggested in the names of Angustias (anguished because she is thirty-nine and not yet married), Magdalena ('tower of strength', 'abundancia de llanto y amor desinteresado'), Amelia (much variety here: 'a district governed by a chieftain', 'honey or the vegetable life of a plant', 'amelioration'), Prudencia ('resignación y sabiduría'), Librada ('liberté') and Paca la Roseta ('l'amoureuse rose') (*7*, 388–9; *13*, 14–15; *17*, 806; *20*, 33, 45; *25*, 92). Some of these suggestions are obviously justified and further illustrate Lorca's poetic response to reality; in others one suspects an excess of academic zeal.

dilemma of repressed vitality, Bernarda Alba's daughters are representative of other 'mujeres en los pueblos de España'. Lorca, then, not only narrows his focus to emphasise vitality and its repression; he also broadens it to show the wider significance of what he presents. Both these things I see as aspects of his poetic vision and technique.

But they are also common to many documentaries and one recalls Lorca's own declaration: *'estos tres actos tienen la intención de un documental fotográfico'* (2). The words have perhaps worried critics unduly. The aim of a documentary is to explore visually a selected aspect of real life. Because of the selection involved — the predetermined subject, the cameraman, the editor — the finished work cannot be wholly realistic. Moreover, like Lorca, the maker of a documentary commonly invites us to find wider significance in what he presents: a pointer perhaps to the degrading effect of social conditions or to the inefficiencies of bureaucracy or to the harmony — or cruelty — of nature, and almost inevitably selection is here accompanied by a special weighting of the evidence in one direction or another. In all this *La casa de Bernarda Alba* can reasonably be likened to documentary.

But there are also differences. In the first place, the maker of a documentary is more clearly confined to specific realities and cannot, like the writer, create characters by taking various elements from different known persons (cf. above, 'Fact and Fiction'). In the second place, despite an almost inevitable bias in the selection of material, one expects the maker of a documentary to subject himself to reality, unlike Lorca who, in his obsession with vitality and its repression, clearly subjects reality to himself. Finally and very especially, the maker of a documentary depends principally on visual communication; for Lorca visual communication is important, but it is on language and on the interplay of language and visual communication that his play most clearly depends. It is this that I propose to study in the following section.

But one final observation is required on significance. Lorca presents a specific reality and invites us to find wider relevance in it. My own inclination is to identify this wider relevance with the subtitle of the play and beyond that with the more general problem of vitality and repression. But significance in a work of art is not easily circumscribed and in the situation of Bernarda's daughters it is tempting to find also, as Rubia Barcia suggests, the image of a Spain closed to the rest of the world, 'una España empeñada en permanecer fiel a una tradición ya moribunda, queriendo perseguir unos ideales que han funcionado en el pasado, pero de imposible resurrección en el presente' (7, 393). The problem arises when, from such general resonances of oppression, critics infer more specific interpretations that the evidence of the play itself shows to be unjustified. A single example must suffice. For Miguel Martínez 'Bernarda es la clase dominante española'; 'lo demás, lo anti-Bernarda, es el pueblo español, en lucha perpetua contra la tiranía', and Adela's final rebellion is 'la rebelión desbordada y excesiva de un pueblo aherrojado' (10, 60—3). This, I suggest, is unacceptable, for it is in conflict with the evidence of the text, where Bernarda epitomises village morality as a whole, independently of class, and 'lo anti-Bernarda' is represented principally by her daughters who belong to the same social class as Bernarda. With *La casa de Bernarda Alba* as with other works of Spanish literature ideological commitment is currently playing havoc with dispassionate criticism.

Intensification

In the preceding pages I have tried to show how Lorca streamlines reality around the theme of vitality and repression. In the present section I aim to illustrate some of the ways in which he emphasises both this duality and the resulting conflict.

In *La casa de Bernarda Alba*, as in *Bodas de sangre* and *Yerma*, the epitome of repression is indicated in the title of the play, emphasis being placed throughout on the barrier that the house offers to the world of vitality outside. Thus, the *'muros gruesos'* of the opening stage direction are later recalled — at the very moment the house is being described as a convent and reference is made to the freedom and joy of the countryside beyond — by the muffled sound of bells from outside *'como a través de varios muros'* (46; cf. also *'lejanísimas'*, 72), and the roof is referred to repeatedly as a frontier between restriction and freedom (61, 75, 85, 87; cf. *35*, 187). Moreover, Lorca's repeated indication that the setting is an interior (3, 34, 67), from which windows are apparently absent except for the audience's own window on the scene, serves as a foil to the insistent emphasis by characters ('mujeres ventaneras', 63) on windows and doors and cracks in doors as means of access to the world outside (5, 17, 18, 23, 28, 30...). For the fact is that Bernarda's house is a prison (cf. the 'voces de presidio' that Adela finally revolts against, 88), confining those within, both grandmother ('encerrada', 4; ' ¡Encerradla! ', 33) and daughters ('viven como metidas en alacenas', 78), and excluding those without (5, 10, 13). As for the reapers' song, with its call to the village women to 'abrir puertas y ventanas', any temptation that we might feel to dismiss it as merely incidental is immediately banished by the way in which Martirio and Adela both seize on the words — the former *'Con nostalgia'*; the second *'Con pasión'* — and thereby demonstrate the relevance to their own situation (49). Similarly, the only other song in the play also calls for freedom — and in similar terms: 'la puerta sola se abrirá' (82), words that are echoed twice in the dialogue that follows (83, 84) to emphasise their dramatic relevance.

The result of so much selective emphasis is that Bernarda's house appears as a symbol of repression. But the evidence so far adduced suggests a type of symbolism very different from that predominating in *Bodas de sangre*. Since I am here touching on an important difference between the two plays, a brief detour is justified. In *Bodas de sangre* the Novia, who has finally yielded to passion and run away with Leonardo, declares:

> ¡Huye!
> Es justo que yo aquí muera
> con los pies dentro del agua
> y espinas en la cabeza.
> Y que me lloren las hojas,
> mujer perdida y doncella.   (II, 651)

'On the one hand she is suffering because she has yielded to her passion and run away with Leonardo ("los pies dentro del agua", "mujer perdida"); on the other hand she is tormented because she continues to struggle against her love ("espinas en la cabeza", "doncella"; cf. "soy limpia...")' (MUP edition, p. xxxviii). The expressions 'los pies dentro del agua' and 'espinas en la cabeza' are obviously symbolic of her situation, but they cannot be interpreted literally, for she does not in fact have her feet in water and she does not literally have a crown of thorns on her head. They have relevant meaning, then, only on the evoked plane, as images of her situation, and can therefore be referred to as monosemic symbols. Bernarda's house, on the other hand, is presented both as a reality and, because of the streamlining and accompanying emphasis on elements of repression, also as a symbol of such repression. It is akin to what T.S. Eliot referred to as the 'objective correlative'. Since we are now invited to accept meaning on two levels, both literal (real plane) and symbolic (evoked plane), the symbols are no longer monosemic but bisemic.[17] The difference can be generalised to *Bodas de sangre* and *La casa de Bernarda Alba* as a whole: whereas the imagery in the former is principally monosemic, that in the latter is predominantly bisemic. It is the essential key to the stylistic difference between the two plays: *Bodas de sangre*, with its mainly monosemic imagery, is obviously poetic and can make little impact on readers or spectators with feet of clay; *La casa de Bernarda Alba*, with its predominantly bisemic imagery, is apparently realistic and therefore has meaning, however limited, even for those who fail to respond to its obvious poetic resonances. This may be one reason for the latter play's wider popularity.

But the distinction is not absolute and in my edition of *Bodas de sangre* I have shown how in certain images in that play 'general resonances are set up *beside* the specific physical reference' (cf. monosemic imagery) and how in others 'the more general resonances develop *around* the specific physical reference' (cf. bisemic imagery) (*op. cit.* xxx). Similarly, in *La casa de Bernarda Alba* it is necessary to supplement my earlier emphasis on bisemic house imagery with pointers also to monosemic imagery where we are presumably not expected to accept a literal meaning, as for example when Bernarda epitomises the imposed eight years of mourning as a bricking up of doors and windows (14), and when Poncia says 'Las viejas vemos a través de las paredes' (42), and in the following exchange between Poncia and Bernarda, in which a monosemic image used by the former is developed by the latter, presumably still in metaphorical terms:

PONCIA.   Pero en cuanto las dejes sueltas [the daughters] se te subirán al tejado.
BERNARDA.   ¡Ya las bajaré tirándoles cantos! (61)

[17] For a study of monosemic and bisemic imagery, with special reference to the poetry of Antonio Machado, see Carlos Bousoño, *Teoría de la expresión literaria*, Gredos, Madrid 1952, pp. 101–50, and, with greater complexity, in the definitive two-volume edition of the same work: Gredos, Madrid 1976, I, 260–360.

But even in these cases of monosemic imagery the evoked plane in *La casa de Bernarda Alba* remains close to the real-life plane of the house itself.

Bernarda's house is characterised not only by its thick walls but also by its whiteness and by the predominance of characters dressed in black. This can be interpreted at various levels. At one level one can see it merely as a reflection of reality, for Andalusian houses are generally whitewashed and adult women in the 1930s were almost invariably dressed in black. But the emphasis on black and white serves not only to reflect reality but also to give an *effect* of reality, and the two things are not necessarily the same. The Hollywood director Sam Fuller has made the point as a general proposition, without reference to Lorca: 'Life is in colour, but black and white is more realistic'.[18] Since documentaries in the 1930s were almost exclusively in black and white, Lorca presumably had this in mind when he declared the documentary intention of his play. But he does not stop at reality and realism. As with the structure of the house he also exploits emotive resonances. The traditional death implication of black is obvious and is made more ominous by association with the solemn, inquisition-like gathering of village women in Act I, fluent in formal religious ritual but lacking in charity (cf. the persecution of La Librada's daughter and references to Bernarda as 'inquisitiva', 31, and to Martirio's interrogation of Adela as 'inquisición', 41). But white, too, appears as an ominous colour in a household where excessive zeal for cleanliness and whitewashing is suggested even in the name of the principal oppressor and culminates — amidst walls now tinged by night and doom — in her order to dress the dead Adela 'como una doncella' (that is, in white). The evidence has been adequately studied and need not detain us, [19] except for two points that are commonly overlooked. First, colour symbolism in Lorca is not a matter of establishing simple equations; it is the overall context that must

[18] *The Observer*, 23 January 1983, p. 45.
[19] *2*, 456–7, 460–1; *8*, 67–8; *21*, 75–6. See also Henryk Ziomek, 'El simbolismo del blanco en *La casa de Bernarda Alba* y en *La dama del alba*', in *Symposium* 24 (1970), 81–5; Janes Frances Spencer, 'El claroscuro en la trilogía lorquiana', in *Cuadernos Americanos* 38, 4 (July–August 1979), 171–87.

guide us. However much the more ominous associations of black may prevail, 'ojos negros' (35) are clearly associated with vitality, and white has similar resonances in ' ¡No quiero perder mi blancura en estas habitaciones!' (29; cf. also the dynamic whiteness of the stallion, 75, and the foam on the sea, 84). Here as elsewhere, what is important in Lorca's colour symbolism is the emotive resonances that colours take on because of the linguistic and dramatic contexts in which they are used. Second point: some of the most powerful effects of Lorca's colour symbolism are produced by contrasts between appearance and reality (as between the *'habitación blanquísima'*, 3, and Magdalena's more metaphorical reference to it, in the same act, as 'esta sala oscura', 15) and by the interplay of contradictory resonances (as when María Josefa's illusioned white sea of foam, 84, is succeeded only a few moments later by the final 'mar de luto', 91). In view of this, the producer of the play might well seek to show in the trousseau wedding sheets that the Alba daughters work on not only pointers to purity and illusion but also to sterility and the final death shroud. Since the imagery is bisemic, producers are usually content to show only sheets.

Lorca uses black and white, then, not only for their documentary value but also for their emotive, poetic potential. But the effect is even greater when colours are made to irrupt into the prevailing panorama of black and white. References to colour, flowers and countryside are relevant, as when Poncia describes Paca la Roseta, with 'una corona de flores en la cabeza', 'lleva[da] a la grupa del caballo hasta lo alto del olivar' (18–19). But it is the visual impact that is most effective: the irruption of discordant colours on stage, as when Adela gives her mother a flowered fan (14), or appears in a green dress (27) or, later, enters with straw on her petticoat (88), or when María Josefa appears *'ataviada con flores en la cabeza y en el pecho'* (32). All are pointers to the denied world of nature outside and they are significantly associated with one or other of the two most rebellious characters in the play. As María Josefa's breakaway to the 'portal de Belén' is anticipated in her flowers, so also Adela's escape to the 'juncos de la orilla' is heralded in her green dress.

Silence fulfils comparable functions to black and white. At one level it can be seen simply as an aspect of reality. But real-life Andalusian houses are not necessarily silent, even when repressed, and the associated impression of austerity – realism in Fuller's sense of the term – is probably more important. From this to the use of silence as an image of repression is but a short distance. It is best illustrated by the arch-oppressor herself. At her first entry she immediately demands silence and repeats her demand on several later occasions where she fears the house's 'buena fachada' is in some way being threatened: 'Chisss' (13), ' ¡Silencio! [...] ¡Silencio digo!' (56), 'Quietas, quietas' (88) and, in the very last words of the play, ' ¡Silencio, silencio he dicho! ¡Silencio!' (91). Finally, silence is used also as a foil to significant sounds. In the opening moments of the play, for example, the sombre tolling of bells is heard amidst 'un gran silencio umbroso' (3). But usually the irruptive sounds point to vitality or revolt: the laughter and 'porrazos' in houses where there are children (46); the shouting and stone-throwing of the reapers and their playing of 'panderos y carrañacas', heard against 'un silencio traspasado por el sol' (47–8); the passions awakened by the stolen photo, beginning with Angustias's irruption on stage, 'furiosa [...] , de modo que haya un gran contraste con los silencios anteriores' (51). Bernarda's reaction in this last case is characteristic: '¡Qué escándalo es éste en mi casa y con el silencio del peso del calor! Estarán las vecinas con el oído pegado a los tabiques' (53). The silence of repression has been momentarily broken and, in her fear that the neighbours may have heard, she sees the 'muros gruesos' as shrunk to mere partition walls. There is a similar duality in Poncia's words to the Criada, ' ¿Tú ves este silencio? Pues hay una tormenta en cada cuarto' (80): silence as repression, amidst which the storm threatens to irrupt. The imagery is exactly comparable to that studied in the previous paragraph: oppressive black and white, with the contrasting irruption of Adela's green dress and María Josefa's flowers.

The above reference to 'una tormenta en cada cuarto' points to another important image: that of heat, with the associated threat of a storm. Physical heat is emphasized from the beginning ('Hace años no he conocido calor igual', 10; cf. Bernarda's call for a fan, 14), and a subtle duality of responses to the stallion's kicking at the wall in Act III juxtaposes physical heat and sexual desire (68): on the one hand Bernarda's merely physical explanation ('Debe tener calor'); on the other hand Prudencia's more comprehending response (' ¿Vais a echarle las potras nuevas? '). In Act II there was a similar duality with Adela, her declared passion for Pepe el Romano ('este fuego que tengo levantado por piernas y boca', 44) being closely followed by a reference to physical heat (45). Heat, then, is an image of desire. But when desire is unsatisfied, heat becomes also an image of torment, and Bernarda's house is appropriately referred to as an 'infierno' (35; cf. also the reference here to a threatening storm). In such a context the symbolism of Martirio's reference to her own suffering from the heat and her desire for the coming of November, 'los días de lluvia, la escarcha; todo lo que no sea este verano interminable' (50), is obvious. But since the words can also be taken literally, it is again bisemic symbolism.

As on a real-life plane thirst is quenched with water, so also, in *La casa de Bernarda Alba*, on a metaphorical plane. Again it is not possible to draw a clear dividing-line. Lorca produces his effects by resonances rather than simple equations. Thus, in Act I an audience will not immediately find symbolic significance in María Josefa's complaint that Bernarda denies her clean drinking-water (16) and may even be inclined to accept Bernarda's reference to the 'maldito pueblo sin río, pueblo de pozos' (14) in an exclusively literal sense. But after the increasing interplay of vitality and repression throughout Acts I and II one can hardly fail to overlook the significance of Adela's thirst in Act III, especially since it reveals itself just as the stallion is kicking at the wall and Bernarda and Prudencia are talking of releasing the fillies for mating. Nor can one overlook the significance of Bernarda's literal response – '(*En voz alta.*) Trae un jarro de agua fresca. (*A Adela.*) Puedes sentarte. (*Adela se sienta.*)' (70) – with its indication of continuing insensitivity and repression. A few moments later it is Martirio who is thirsty (77); then Adela again (81). 'Voy a beber agua', she says, and this, in context, recalls the earlier image of her passion for El Romano, 'Mirando sus ojos me parece que bebo su sangre lentamente' (44). Water, then, is a pointer to sexual satisfaction and, thence also, to freedom from restraints imposed by the house, as in María Josefa's repeated clamour to escape to the 'orilla del mar' (33, 82, 84) and her emphasis on waves and foam (84). But it is also a pointer to the power of passion and the unstoppable flow of life, as when Prudencia says 'dejo que el agua corra' (68) and when La Poncia sums up Bernarda's obstinate blindness with the words 'Cuando una no puede con el mar lo más fácil es volver las espaldas para no verlo' (80). In short, water is another image of vitality. The village itself changes its topography to make the point. At the beginning of the play it was a 'maldito pueblo sin río, pueblo de pozos' (14); by the end Adela's revolt has given it also 'juncos' and 'orilla' (87). Moreover, these 'juncos' remind us that vegetation too is commonly associated with vitality in *La casa de Bernarda Alba*: the fields with their 'alegría' (47), the 'olivar' as a place of love (18, 47), 'árboles quemados' as an image of the reapers (47), the 'ramos del portal de Belén' as an object of María Josefa's longing (82) and the 'hierbas' as an image of what Bernarda is keen to exclude from her house (78). One finds something similar with air (14, 35, 60, 72) and animals (7, 14, 15, 34, 50, 68, 81–2, 89), and Bernarda is correspondingly keen to banish them: 'no ha de entrar en esta casa el viento de la calle' (14), 'Igual que si hubiera pasado por ella una manada de cabras' (14; cf. her desire to exclude the stallion).

The above images of vitality are most commonly enticements – and threats – from outside and are therefore denied to the Alba daughters. 'Hilo y aguja para las hembras. Látigo y mula para el varón. Eso tiene la gente que nace con posibles' (15). Whereas the man's life is associated with nature's dynamism and with corresponding moral freedom, the woman's life is circumscribed by the man-made prison of the home, with needlework as her principal occupation and, ultimately, the most expressive image of her existence. It is something common to other Lorca plays. Moreover, as in some of those other plays, needlework not only epitomises the woman's repressed life; it also appears as a means by which, albeit vainly, she seeks some form of escape from her confinement: Mariana Pineda by embroidering a banner for the Liberal cause, Yerma by making children's clothes, the Alba daughters by working at their trousseaus. The gypsy nun in *Romancero gitano*, embroidering modest flowers on an altar cloth and dreaming of the more exotic flowers that she would like to embroider, is not notably different. In each case the futile or frustrated illusion serves to bring out even more clearly the cruelty of the repression.

Needlework, of course, is a sedentary occupation: '*Las hijas de Bernarda están sentadas en sillas bajas, cosiendo*' (34). It is therefore a short distance from needlework to sitting itself, and this, too, is emphasised by Lorca as a pointer to repression. There are several examples, but the following is the clearest. Bells have just been heard '*como a través de varios muros*' as the men go back to their work in the fields:

ADELA.   (*Sentándose.*)   ¡Ay, quién pudiera salir también a los
campos!
MAGDALENA. (*Sentándose.*)   ¡Cada clase tiene que hacer lo suyo!
MARTIRIO. (*Sentándose.*)   ¡Así es!
AMELIA. (*Sentándose.*)   ¡Ay!
PONCIA.   No hay alegría como la de los campos en esta época. (47)

With sitting, as with needlework, the significant indications are contained not only — or even principally — in the words spoken, but
also in the stage directions and consequently, in any adequate production, in the actions and movements of the characters. Similarly
with the repeated '*Pausa*' (51) to bring out Martirio's hesitation
about whether she should tell Amelia more about her suspicions,
and with the often repeated '*Con intención*' (together with other
similar tonal guides: '*Con sorna*', '*Con crueldad*', '*Con odio*'...) to
emphasise the emotive resonances of what is said and, very especially,
the increasing bitterness of relationships in the Alba household. It is
an aspect of Lorca's theatre that is commonly overlooked, especially
in amateur productions. In a mature Lorca play elements are significantly streamlined and orchestrated into an evolving poetic whole,
with a subtle gradation of tension and imagery according to the
demands of each successive moment. As Lorca himself said, there
are no 'drops' of poetry in this work. Because of the skilful integration of its parts the whole work is a poem, from beginning to
end.

A final point must be made: about Lorca's use of the chorus in
Bodas de sangre and *La casa de Bernarda Alba*. In the former its
presence is obvious, especially in the third act where a succession of
unreal, stylised personages appear and comment on the action,
essentialising it, emphasising its inevitability, universalising the
drama and veiling the harshness of the action in a tone of lyrical
lamentation. It is something that we most associate with classical
Greek tragedy, and at first sight it is tempting to assume that *La casa
de Bernarda Alba* has no chorus.[20] In fact, the function of the

---

[20] In this respect Miralles (*Archivum* 21, 1971, 84) seems to con-
fuse chorus as a commentary on the action ('ilustradora del suceso
dramático') with chorus in a more operatic sense, and, guided presumably by the latter, finds choruses only in the litany for the dead
husband (12–13) and in the song of the reapers (48–9).

chorus in this play is fulfilled most notably by María Josefa, whose perceptive madness helps to give her the uninhibited detachment and lucidity that one associates with the chorus of Greek tragedy, and, even more clearly, by Poncia and the Criada in their important exchange in the middle of Act III (80–1), shortly before the dramatic climax of the play. It is the latter that I take as my illustration. No sooner has Bernarda left than Poncia sums up and universalises Bernarda's attitude: 'Cuando una no puede con el mar lo más fácil es volver las espaldas para no verlo' and the Criada supplements her observation. Thereupon Poncia reviews her own futile attempt to warn of the approaching danger, epitomises the situation of the household in characteristic imagery and foretells the outcome. Again the Criada comments on Bernarda's attitude and Poncia proceeds to place the action of the play as a wider context, both temporal ('el año pasado ...') and human ('Un hombre es un hombre'), to which indications are added on Adela's affair with Pepe. 'No sé lo que va a pasar aquí', says the Criada, and Poncia, with further universalising imagery, expresses her desire to escape from this 'casa de guerra'. Perhaps nothing will happen, suggests the maid, but Poncia knows that things have gone too far. Martirio, of course, will play a key role in the outcome and her character is appropriately summarised. This prompts the Criada to find the daughters all bad, whereupon Poncia puts her finger on the essential problem: 'Son mujeres sin hombre, nada más. En estas cuestiones se olvida hasta la sangre' – a nice anticipation of Martirio's 'Mi sangre ya no es la tuya' to Adela a few moments later. The case, I suggest, is clear. This is no mere incidental, real-life gossiping of minor characters. By their notable concentration on the essentials of the conflict, by Poncia's emphasis on the inevitably tragic outcome and by the repeated reference to both conflict and outcome as part of a universal pattern, they fulfil exactly the same function as the Woodcutters in *Bodas de sangre*. But there are differences, too: in the lesser invocation of nature's involvement in the tragedy, in the lesser abundance of monosemic imagery, and, most clearly of all, in the fact that Poncia and the Criada, unlike the Woodcutters, are real-life characters fully integrated into the total action of the play. Whereas the Woodcutters, like the Moon and Beggar Death and the Spinning Girls, are akin to monosemic images, with significance almost exclusively on the evoked plane, as choruses, Poncia and the Criada are akin to bisemic images, existing both as real-life maids and as tragic chorus. Their role is not therefore less poetic; it is, however, less obviously lyrical. Perhaps Lorca had this in mind when he declared, in 1936: 'El teatro que ha perdurado siempre es el de los poetas. Siempre ha estado el teatro en manos de los poetas. Y ha sido mejor el teatro en tanto más grande el poeta. No es — claro — el poeta lírico, sino el poeta dramático' (II, 1046).

'LA OBRA MAS PERFECTA'?

It is commonly asserted that *La casa de Bernarda Alba* is Lorca's greatest play, 'la más intensa y lograda de [sus] obras',[21] even that it is the greatest play in modern Spanish literature, 'la obra más lograda y profunda del teatro español moderno' (7, 386). Given the outstanding quality of other works by Lorca and of certain plays by other modern Spanish dramatists, I find myself scarcely more able to express an opinion on this than I can about whether Shakespeare's *Hamlet* is greater or less great than his *Antony and Cleopatra*. Nor do I know of any critical study that has either demonstrated or refuted the validity of such statements. Present-day critical esteem rests rather heavily on the criterion of social commitment, as when Rubia Barcia, immediately after the words quoted above, draws attention to the play's 'posible y casi inevitable dimensión social' and proceeds to explore its relevance to such 'doctrinas sistemáticas y excluyentes' as Communism, Fascism and Naziism (7, 386).[22] Since I myself am unable to accept that social commitment necessarily enhances the value of a work of art and find that current emphasis on such commitment unduly narrows one's critical focus, since I am also doubtful whether human dilemmas

[21] Angel Valbuena Prat, *Historia del teatro español*, Noguer, Barcelona 1956, p. 646.

[22] The point is demonstrated most clearly in two excellent surveys of Lorca's fortunes — and misfortunes — at the hands of Spanish post-Civil War playwrights and critics: Antonio Buero Vallejo, *Tres maestros ante el público*, Alianza, Madrid 1973, pp. 97–164 ('García Lorca ante el esperpento' [1971]), and Robert G. Sánchez, 'Lorca, the post-war theater and the conflict of generations', in *Kentucky Romance Quarterly* 19 (1972), 17–29.

arise solely, or even principally, from what is generally understood by social pressures, I lack this touchstone of esteem and, in the preceding pages, having analysed the profoundly *human* dilemma presented, I have placed my main emphasis on less thematic criteria such as the expressiveness of the various elements used and the manner of their integration into a coherent and dynamically progressing whole. Though the evidence does not enable me to measure the play against other outstanding works of the modern Spanish theatre, it leaves me in no doubt that *La casa de Bernarda Alba* is a truly great work and one of Lorca's masterpieces.

But there is perhaps a difference between greatness and perfection. 'La mayoría de la crítica', says García Posada, 'la considera la obra más perfecta del teatro lorquiano.'[23] If they do — and I am by no means certain of this — the criteria of relevance, integration and expressiveness that have been emphasized throughout this study compel me to disagree. *La casa de Bernarda Alba*, I suggest, is not Lorca's most perfect play.

I draw attention first to two elements that I believe detract from the streamlined intensity of the work: first, the Criada's outburst in Act I about social oppression (8), which I find misdirects our attention, at an important moment of exposition, from the main theme of the play; secondly, Prudencia's presence at the beginning of Act III, which disrupts the effect of claustrophobic seclusion from the world outside. Moreover, in the latter case real-life experience itself is violated, for no sooner has Prudencia said 'Os he hecho una visita larga' than Bernarda asks about Prudencia's husband, and Prudencia, shortly afterwards, enquires about progress with Angustias's wedding arrangements. What, then, have they been talking about during this 'visita larga'? In Spain custom and courtesy both demand — especially in rural areas — that one's first enquiries should be about the well-being and latest news of those one visits or is visited by and of their immediate family. One can see positive reasons for Prudencia's presence — a different response to the sort of problem with which Bernarda is faced and a relaxation of tension after the end of Act II — but one still regrets the weaknesses.

I find a similar violation of real-life experience in Poncia's observation, after thirty years in the household, 'Angustias ya debe tener mucho más de los treinta', and Bernarda's reply, 'Treinta y nueve justos' (20). It is useful information for the audience, but the way in which it is given produces a sense of shock that one does not normally associate with Lorca's writings and it is not certain that this is completely dispelled by emphasis on Poncia's 'game of dual intent' (above, xlii n.). One might be tempted to say something similar also of Poncia's and the Criada's exposition in the opening minutes of the play, but I myself feel less disadvantage at this point and suspect that Lorca was deliberately exploiting conventions of the realist theatre — as he had formerly exploited conventions of the puppet theatre and as he planned to exploit conventions of *zarzuela* (*34*, 46) — as a preliminary to showing how this theatrical form, too, could be incorporated into his own poetic world. An audience, I think, accepts such conventions, especially when the author exploits them consciously (cf. 'el artificio del ingenio' which Lorca declared openly in the prologue to *La zapatera prodigiosa*). The problem, for me at least, arises only when Lorca has proceeded from this initial convention, elevated realistic action to a higher plane of symbolism in which elements are integrated into an evolving poetic whole, and then, as in the above Poncia—Bernarda and Prudencia—Bernarda exchanges, lapses into fragments of non-symbolic (that is, non-bisemic) realism which oblige us to test the words by reference to real-life experience. It may well be that he would have eliminated such weaknesses if he had lived longer, for he rarely failed to revise his works and often made changes even during rehearsals. Regrettably he had no opportunity to revise *La casa de Bernarda Alba*.

Though these apparent blemishes could be eliminated with little difficulty, it is less sure that the next one could. Thick walls, black and white, silence, sewing and sitting — all contribute to the overall effect of repression. This effect is disrupted, however, by what I believe to be the excessive coming and going of the characters. Again there are positive reasons for this: to allow for important exchanges between Bernarda and Poncia (18–21, 56–61, 77–9), Poncia and Adela (42–4) and Martirio and Adela (63–4, 85–8) that could hardly take place while the other characters are onstage. So much movement does, however, make it difficult for the producer to bring out a static effect as part of the overall claustrophobic atmosphere. The problem can most easily be circumvented in a television production where the audience may be made less aware of exits and entrances. Onstage, I find, the best response is to emphasise movement as a manifestation of nervous restlessness and thus to use it as a pointer to the heralded 'tormenta'. But whereas the threat of the storm grows — and the white walls become progressively less white — the movements are fairly consistent throughout the play. It is a weakness that I have not seen countered in production with the care that it deserves.

My inference from the above — and from the evidence of staging difficulties experienced by Juan Antonio Bardem (*4*) and Farris Anderson (*19*) — is that, though *La casa de Bernarda Alba* is a remarkable play by any standards, Lorca did not wholly succeed in reconciling realism and realistic techniques with his own essentially poetic vision. This raises again the question of his dramatic development and perhaps throws doubt on the commonly expressed view of *La casa de Bernarda Alba* as a pointer to the sort of play that he would have written, had he lived longer. Within the 'tierra española' trilogy itself the progression towards increasing realism and greater social commitment is evident, and statements in interviews suggest that this was part of a more general development in his writing. Lorca's brother, however, a sensitive critic, has argued against this: one should not infer from the greater realism of *La casa de Bernarda Alba* that Lorca would necessarily have continued along this line; just as there was a transition in his poetry 'desde la desolada visión negativa de *Poeta en Nueva York* al lirismo, de tonalidad granadina, del *Diván del Tamarit*', so also one finds evidence of a similar change in his writing for the theatre: notably in *Los sueños de mi prima Aurelia*, a play that he was working on during the last weeks of his life. 'De la dura objetivación del mundo de Bernarda se pasa a una tierna evocación intimista; el personaje principal de la obra es el propio Federico niño y la participación del verso es capital' (*28*, 373—4). Given the constant process of experimentation in Lorca's writings, both poetry and drama, and his extraordinary openness to inspiration and techniques from very different sources, both popular and sophisticated — *cante jondo*, *creacionismo*, puppet theatre, the popular *romance*, children's nursery rhymes, surrealism, Persian and Arabic poetry, etc. —, I find this argument extremely suggestive. Lorca disliked being pigeon-holed

('No quiero que me encasillen', II, 1232) and commonly had mis-givings about a work by the time it appeared. Moreover, *La casa de Bernarda Alba* itself, I have suggested, was perhaps merely an experi-ment with realistic techniques, exactly comparable to his earlier experiments with techniques of the puppet theatre. Finally, Lorca himself, in 1936, made it clear that realism was not his ultimate aim:

> Yo en el teatro he seguido una trayectoria definida. Mis primeras comedias son irrepresentables. Ahora creo que una de ellas, *Así que pasen cinco años*, va a ser representada por el Club Anfistora. En estas comedias imposibles está mi verdadero propósito. Pero para demostrar una personalidad y tener derecho al respeto he dado otras cosas. (II, 1079)

In view of the prevailing critical emphasis on realism and social awareness and the consequent special favour accorded to *La casa de Bernarda Alba*, it is salutory to recall that Lorca himself, at a time of increasing realism and social awareness in Spanish literature, perhaps saw this play merely as one of those 'otras cosas' '[dadas] para demostrar una personalidad y tener derecho al respeto'. Whether this be so or not, it is a remarkable work. But so are half a dozen more of his plays, and as many more collections of his poetry. To see Lorca's evolution as directed exclusively towards a form of expression that currently enjoys special favour is to channel his genius too narrowly. The range and quality of his writings up to the time of his death — two months after his thirty-eighth birthday — overwhelms one with the thought of what he might still have written and reduces one to silence.

SELECTED BIBLIOGRAPHY

In the present edition, references to Lorca's works other than *La casa de Bernarda Alba* are to his *Obras completas*, 2 vols., Aguilar, Madrid 1977. The following critical studies are listed in chronological order of first publication. In all cases *La casa de Bernarda Alba* is abbreviated to *CBA*.

1. Eric Bentley, *In Search of Theater*, Knopf, New York 1953, pp. 215–32 ('The Poet in Dublin'). Spanish translation: 'El poeta en Dublín (García Lorca)', in *Asomante* 9, 2 (April–June 1953), 44–58 [*CBA* production problems at the Abbey Theatre; similarities to Ibsen].

2. Sumner M. Greenfield, 'Poetry and stagecraft in *CBA*', in *Hispania* 38 (1955), 456–61 [Symbolic use of white; function of María Josefa and the villagers].

3. G. Torrente Ballester, *Teatro español contemporáneo*, Guardarrama, Madrid, 1957, pp. 111–26 ('Bernarda Alba y sus hijas, o un mundo sin perdón') [Dominant Bernarda, psychologically convincing, versus her more abstract daughters, 'el instinto sexual en forma pura y primitiva'].

4. Juan Antonio Bardem, '*CBA*', in *Primer Acto* 50 (February 1964 [incorrectly dated 1963]), 8–11 [Production problems].

5. Robert Lima, *The Theatre of García Lorca*, Las Américas, New York 1963, 263–87 ('*CBA*') [Comprehensive survey with emphasis on fate].

6. Alberto del Monte, 'Il realismo de *CBA*', in *Belfagor* 20 (1965), 130–48 [Left-wing social commitment in Lorca and class-based repression in *CBA*].

7. J. Rubia Barcia, 'El realismo "mágico" de *CBA*', in *Revista Hispánica Moderna* 31 (1965), 385–98 [Realism and poetry in *CBA*].

8. R.A. Young, 'García Lorca's *CBA*: a microcosm of Spanish culture', in *Modern Languages* 50 (1969), 66–72 [Emphasises oppressive tradition, especially the Spanish equation of honour with reputation].

9. Judith M. Bull, '"Santa Bárbara" and *CBA*', in *Bulletin of Hispanic Studies* 47 (1970), 117–23 [Elucidates a specific passage; see Endnote G].

10. Miguel A. Martínez, 'Realidad y símbolo en *CBA*', in *Revista de Estudios Hispánicos* 4 (1970), 55–66 [Village, characters and conflict as symbols of Spain].

11. Cedric Busette, *Obra dramática de García Lorca*, Las Américas, New York 1971, pp. 78–111 (*'CBA'*) [Fate as the driving force].

12. Roberto G. Sánchez, 'La última manera dramática de García Lorca (Hacia una clarificación de lo "social" en su teatro)', in *Papeles de Son Armadans* 60 (January–March 1971), 83–102 [Lorca's late 'postura crítica' involves both an ideological shift and an Ibsen-inspired artistic change].

13. Medardo Fraile, 'An introduction to *CBA*', in *Vida Hispánica* 22, 1 (Winter 1974), 5–15 [General survey with emphasis on characters].

14. Carole Slade, 'The hell of Bernarda's house', in *García Lorca Review* 3 (1975), 70–8 [Imagery of hell; cf. Dante's *Inferno*].

15. Virginia Higginbotham, *The Comic Spirit of Federico García Lorca*, University of Texas Press, Austin–London 1976, pp. 111–19 (*'CBA'*) [Bernarda as caricature].

16. María Eugenia March de Orti, 'El "doble fondo" de *CBA*', in *Homenaje a Andrés Iduarte*, ed. J. Alazraki, R. Grass, R.O. Salmon, The American Hispanist, Clear Creek, Indiana, 1976, 257–70 [Principally outline with a touch of Jungian psychology].

17. Wilma Newberry, 'Patterns of negation in *CBA*', in *Hispania* 59 (1976), 802–9 [Synthesis of anti-vital elements].

18. Nina M. Scott, 'Sight and insight in *CBA*', in *Revista de Estudios Hispánicos* 10 (1976), 297–308 [Importance of perception – and blindness – in *CBA*].

19. Farris Anderson, *'CBA*: problems in Act One', in *García Lorca Review* 5 (1977), 66–80 [Staging difficulties].

20. Sumner M. Greenfield, 'Lorca's theatre: a synthetic reexamination', in *Journal of Spanish Studies: Twentieth Century* 5 (1977), 31–46 [A good synthesis and a much-needed rejoinder to those who overplay ideological commitment].

21. Allen Josephs and Juan Caballero, Introduction to their edition of *CBA*, Cátedra, Madrid 1977 [Comprehensive study of *CBA* in the context of Lorca's theatre].

22. Roberto C. Spires, 'Linguistic codes and dramatic action in *CBA*', in *The American Hispanist* 3, 28 (January 1978), 7–11 [Poncia as the key character in a dramatic struggle that stems from the underlying social system].

23. Vicente Cabrera, 'Poetic structure in Lorca's *CBA*', in *Hispania* 61 (1978), 466–71 [Symbolic and structural elements].

24. Vicente Cabrera, 'Cristo y el infierno en *CBA*', in *Revista de Estudios Hispánicos* 13 (1979), 135–42 [Religious imagery gives poetic structure to the work].

25. James Dauphiné, 'Le réalisme symbolique dans *CBA*', in *Les Langues Néo-Latines* 73, iv (October–December 1979), 85–96 [Reality elevated via symbol to wider significance].

26. Mac E. Barrick, '"Los antiguos sabían muchas cosas": superstition in *CBA*', in *Hispanic Review* 48 (1980), 469–77 [The use of popular superstitions as pointers to the outcome].

27. Gwynne Edwards, *Lorca. The Theatre beneath the Sand*, Marion Boyars, London–Boston 1980, pp. 234–76, 292–6 (*'The House of Bernarda Alba'*) [A comprehensive survey].

28. Francisco García Lorca, *Federico y su mundo* [1980], 2nd ed., Alianza, Madrid 1981, pp. 372–97 (*'CBA'*) [Fact and fiction; Lorca's use of space and time].

29. Isaac Rubio, 'Notas sobre el realismo de *CBA*, de García Lorca', in *Revista Canadiense de Estudios Hispánicos* 4 (1980), 169–82 [Finds realism in the emphasis on social and economic forces].

30. Richard A. Seybolt, 'Characterization in *CBA*: the case of Martirio', in *García Lorca Review* 8 (1980), 82–90 [Martirio as a 'uniquely complicated and "human" personality'].

31. Barry E. Weingarten, 'Bernarda Alba: nature as unnatural', in *The World of Nature in the Works of Federico García Lorca*, ed. Joseph W. Zdenek, Winthrop Studies on Major Modern Writers, Rock Hill, South Carolina, 1980, pp. 129–38 [Bernarda's struggle to dominate nature].

32. Robin W. Fiddian, 'Adelaida's story and the cyclical design of *CBA*', in *Romance Notes* 21 (1980–1), 150–4 [Thematic foreshadowing and patterns of repetition].

33. Alfredo Rodríguez, 'Bernarda Alba, creation as defiance', in *Romance Notes* 21 (1980–1), 279–82 [Lorca consciously upturns the tradition of man as the defender of family honour].

34. Mario Hernández, Introduction and notes to his manuscript-based edition of *CBA*, Alianza, Madrid 1981 [Good contextual information].

35. Leo Hickey, 'Culturology and cumulativeness in *CBA*', in *Quinquereme* 5 (1982), 186–95 [House symbolism; cultural and biological forces].

LA CASA DE
BERNARDA ALBA

DRAMA DE MUJERES EN
LOS PUEBLOS DE ESPAÑA
(1936)

PERSONAS

BERNARDA, 60 años
MARÍA JOSEFA (madre de Bernarda), 80 años
ANGUSTIAS (hija de Bernarda), 39 años*
MAGDALENA (hija de Bernarda), 30 años
AMELIA (hija de Bernarda), 27 años
MARTIRIO (hija de Bernarda), 24 años
ADELA (hija de Bernarda), 20 años
LA PONCIA (criada), 60 años
CRIADA, 50 años
PRUDENCIA, 50 años
MENDIGA
MUJER 1.ª
MUJER 2.ª
MUJER 3.ª
MUJER 4.ª
MUCHACHA
MUJERES DE LUTO

El poeta advierte que estos tres actos tienen la intención de un documental fotográfico.

*Sic in Losada and Aguilar; ms: 36 años, belied by p. 20.

ACTO PRIMERO [1]

Habitación blanquísima del interior de la casa de Bernarda. Muros gruesos. Puertas en arco con cortinas de yute rematadas con madroños y volantes.[2] Sillas de anea. Cuadros con paisajes inverosímiles de ninfas o reyes de leyenda. Es verano. Un gran silencio umbroso se extiende por la escena. Al levantarse el telón está la escena sola. Se oyen doblar las campanas.

(*Sale la Criada.*)

CRIADA
Ya tengo el doble de esas campanas metido entre las sienes.

LA PONCIA (*Sale comiendo pan y chorizo.*)
Llevan ya más de dos horas de gori-gori. Han venido curas de todos los pueblos. La iglesia está hermosa. En el primer responso se desmayó la Magdalena.

CRIADA
Esa es la que se queda más sola.

PONCIA
Era a la única que quería el padre. ¡Ay! ¡Gracias a Dios que estamos solas un poquito! Yo he venido a comer.

---

[1] Introduction, p. ix.
[2] *Arched doorways with hessian curtains edged with tassels and flounces.*

CRIADA

   ¡Si te viera Bernarda!

PONCIA

   ¡Quisiera que ahora, como no come ella, que todas nos muriéramos de hambre! ¡Mandona! ¡Dominanta! ¡Pero se fastidia! Le he abierto la orza de chorizos.

CRIADA (*Con tristeza ansiosa.*)

   ¿Por qué no me das para mi niña, Poncia?

PONCIA

   Entra y llévate también un puñado de garbanzos.[3] ¡Hoy no se dará cuenta!

VOZ (*Dentro.*)

   ¡Bernarda!

PONCIA

   La vieja. ¿Está bien encerrada?

CRIADA

   Con dos vueltas de llave.

PONCIA

   Pero debes poner también la tranca. Tiene unos dedos como cinco ganzúas.

VOZ

   ¡Bernarda!

PONCIA (*A voces.*)

   ¡Ya viene! (*A la Criada.*) Limpia bien todo. Si Bernarda no ve relucientes las cosas me arrancará los pocos pelos que me quedan.

CRIADA

   ¡Qué mujer!

---

[3] *a fistful of chickpeas* (a staple Spanish food).

PONCIA

Tirana de todos los que la rodean. Es capaz de sentarse encima
de tu corazón y ver cómo te mueres durante un año sin que se
le cierre esa sonrisa fría que lleva en su maldita cara. ¡Limpia,
limpia ese vidriado!

CRIADA

Sangre en las manos tengo de fregarlo todo.

PONCIA

Ella la más aseada, ella la más decente, ella la más alta. Buen
descanso ganó su pobre marido.

(*Cesan las campanas.*)

CRIADA

¿Han venido todos sus parientes?

PONCIA

Los de ella. La gente de él la odia. Vinieron a verlo muerto, y
le hicieron la cruz.

CRIADA

¿Hay bastantes sillas?

PONCIA

Sobran. Que se sienten en el suelo. Desde que murió el padre de
Bernarda no han vuelto a entrar las gentes bajo estos techos.
Ella no quiere que la vean en su dominio. ¡Maldita sea!

CRIADA

Contigo se portó bien.

PONCIA

Treinta años lavando sus sábanas, treinta años comiendo sus
sobras, noches en vela cuando tose, días enteros mirando por
la rendija para espiar a los vecinos y llevarle el cuento; vida

sin secretos una con otra, y sin embargo, ¡maldita sea!, ¡mal dolor de clavo le pinche en los ojos! [4]

CRIADA

¡Mujer!

PONCIA

Pero yo soy buena perra: ladro cuando me lo dice y muerdo los talones de los que piden limosna cuando ella me azuza;[5] mis hijos trabajan en sus tierras y ya están los dos casados, pero un día me hartaré.

CRIADA

Y ese día...

PONCIA

Ese día me encerraré con ella en un cuarto y le estaré escupiendo un año entero: 'Bernarda, por esto, por aquello, por lo otro', hasta ponerla como un lagarto machacado por los niños, que es lo que es ella y toda su parentela. Claro es que no le envidio la vida. Le quedan cinco mujeres, cinco hijas feas, que quitando a Angustias, la mayor, que es la hija del primer marido y tiene dineros, las demás, mucha puntilla bordada, muchas camisas de hilo, pero pan y uvas por toda herencia.[6]

CRIADA

¡Ya quisiera tener yo lo que ellas!

PONCIA

Nosotras tenemos nuestras manos y un hoyo en la tierra de la verdad.[7]

---

[4] *Red-hot nails* (lit. *May agony of nail*) *pierce her eyes.* A popular low-class expression.

[5] *But I'm a good dog. I bark when she tells me to and snap at the heels of those who come begging when she sets me on them.*

[6] *the rest, lots of frills* (strictly *broderie anglaise*), *lots of linen shifts* (underskirts), *but bread and grapes as their only inheritance.*

[7] *a hole in God's acre. Hoyo* and *tierra de la verdad* are commonly used to indicate *grave* and *cemetery* respectively.

CRIADA

Esa es la única tierra que nos dejan a los que no tenemos nada.

PONCIA (*En la alacena.*)

Este cristal tiene unas motas.

CRIADA

Ni con el jabón ni con bayeta se le quitan.

(*Suenan las campanas.*)

PONCIA

El último responso. Me voy a oírlo. A mí me gusta mucho cómo canta el párroco. En el 'Pater Noster' subió, subió, subió la voz que parecía un cántaro llenándose de agua poco a poco. ¡Claro es que al final dio un gallo, pero da gloria oírlo! Ahora que nadie como el antiguo sacristán, Tronchapinos. En la misa de mi madre, que esté en gloria, cantó. Retumbaban las paredes, y cuando decía amén era como si un lobo hubiese entrado en la iglesia. (*Imitándolo.*) ¡Améééén. (*Se echa a toser.*)

CRIADA

Te vas a hacer el gaznate polvo.[8]

PONCIA

¡Otra cosa hacía polvo yo! [8] (*Sale riendo.*)

(*La Criada limpia. Suenan las campanas.*)

CRIADA (*Llevando el canto.*)

Tin, tin, tan. Tin, tin, tan. ¡Dios lo haya perdonado!

MENDIGA (*Con una niña.*)

¡Alabado sea Dios!

CRIADA

Tin, tin, tan. ¡Que nos espere muchos años! Tin, tin, tan.

---

[8] *'You'll be straining your windpipe.' 'I'd rather be straining something else.'*

MENDIGA (*Fuerte con cierta irritación.*)
   ¡Alabado sea Dios!

CRIADA (*Irritada.*)
   ¡Por siempre!

MENDIGA
   Vengo por las sobras.

   (*Cesan las campanas.*)

CRIADA
   Por la puerta se va a la calle. Las sobras de hoy son para mí.

MENDIGA
   Mujer, tú tienes quien te gane.[9] Mi niña y yo estamos solas.

CRIADA
   También están solos los perros y viven.

MENDIGA
   Siempre me las dan.

CRIADA
   Fuera de aquí. ¿Quién os dijo que entrarais? Ya me habéis dejado los pies señalados. (*Se van. Limpia.*) Suelos barnizados con aceite, alacenas, pedestales, camas de acero, para que traguemos quina las que vivimos en las chozas de tierra con un plato y una cuchara.[10] ¡Ojalá que un día no quedáramos ni uno para contarlo! (*Vuelven a sonar las campanas.*) Sí, sí, ¡vengan clamores!, ¡venga caja con filos dorados y toallas de seda para llevarla!; ¡que lo mismo estarás tú que estaré yo![11] Fastídiate, Antonio María Benavides, tieso con tu traje de paño y tus botas enterizas. ¡Fastídiate! ¡Ya no volverás a levantarme las enaguas detrás de la puerta de tu corral!

---

[9] *you have someone to provide for you.*
[10] Endnote A.
[11] Endnote B.

(*Por el fondo, de dos en dos, empiezan a entrar mujeres de luto con pañuelos grandes, faldas y abanicos negros. Entran lentamente hasta llenar la escena.*)

CRIADA (*Rompiendo a gritar.*)

¡Ay Antonio María Benavides, que ya no verás estas paredes, ni comerás el pan de esta casa! Yo fui la que más te quiso de las que te sirvieron. (*Tirándose del cabello.*) ¿Y he de vivir yo después de haberte marchado? ¿Y he de vivir?

(*Terminan de entrar las doscientas mujeres y aparece Bernarda y sus cinco hijas. Bernarda viene apoyada en un bastón.*)[12]

BERNARDA (*A la Criada.*)

¡Silencio!

CRIADA (*Llorando.*)

¡Bernarda!

BERNARDA

Menos gritos y más obras. Debías haber procurado que todo esto estuviera más limpio para recibir al duelo. Vete. No es éste tu lugar. (*La Criada se va sollozando.*) Los pobres son como los animales. Parece como si estuvieran hechos de otras sustancias.

MUJER 1.ª

Los pobres sienten también sus penas.

BERNARDA

Pero las olvidan delante de un plato de garbanzos.

MUCHACHA (*Con timidez.*)

Comer es necesario para vivir.

BERNARDA

A tu edad no se habla delante de las personas mayores.

MUJER 1.ª

Niña, cállate.

[12] Endnote C.

BERNARDA

No he dejado que nadie me dé lecciones. Sentarse.

(*Se sientan. Pausa.*)

(*Fuerte.*) Magdalena, no llores. Si quieres llorar te metes debajo de la cama. ¿Me has oído?

MUJER 2.ª (*A Bernarda.*)

¿Habéis empezado los trabajos en la era?

BERNARDA

Ayer.

MUJER 3.ª

Cae el sol como plomo.

MUJER 1.ª

Hace años no he conocido calor igual.

(*Pausa. Se abanican todas.*)

BERNARDA

¿Está hecha la limonada?

PONCIA (*Sale con una gran bandeja llena de jarritas blancas, que distribuye.*)

Sí, Bernarda.

BERNARDA

Dale a los hombres.

PONCIA

La están tomando en el patio.

BERNARDA

Que salgan por donde han entrado. No quiero que pasen por aquí.

MUCHACHA (*A Angustias.*)

Pepe el Romano estaba con los hombres del duelo.

ANGUSTIAS

Allí estaba.

BERNARDA
Estaba su madre. Ella ha visto a su madre. A Pepe no lo ha visto ni ella ni yo.

MUCHACHA
Me pareció...

BERNARDA
Quien sí estaba era el viudo de Darajalí.[13] Muy cerca de tu tía. A ése lo vimos todas.

MUJER 2.ª (*Aparte y en voz baja.*)
¡Mala, más que mala!

MUJER 3.ª (*Aparte y en voz baja.*)
¡Lengua de cuchillo!

BERNARDA
Las mujeres en la iglesia no deben mirar más hombre que al oficiante, y a ése porque tiene faldas. Volver la cabeza es buscar el calor de la pana.

MUJER 1.ª (*En voz baja.*)
¡Vieja lagarta recocida! [14]

PONCIA (*Entre dientes.*)
¡Sarmentosa por calentura de varón! [15]

BERNARDA (*Dando un golpe de bastón en el suelo.*)
Alabado sea Dios.[16]

TODAS (*Santiguándose.*)
Sea por siempre bendito y alabado.

---

[13] A hamlet in the province of Granada (*21*, 125).
[14] Endnote D.
[15] *Viny old creeper after a man's heat!* (a silent quester after heat like a vine shoot [*sarmiento*]).
[16] On the litany that follows, see Endnote E.

BERNARDA

Descansa en paz con la santa
compaña de cabecera.

TODAS

¡Descansa en paz!

BERNARDA

Con el ángel San Miguel
y su espada justiciera.

TODAS

¡Descansa en paz!

BERNARDA

Con la llave que todo lo abre
y la mano que todo lo cierra.

TODAS

¡Descansa en paz!

BERNARDA

Con los bienaventurados
y las lucecitas del campo.

TODAS

¡Descansa en paz!

BERNARDA

Con nuestra santa caridad
y las almas de tierra y mar.

TODAS

¡Descansa en paz!

BERNARDA

Concede el reposo a tu siervo Antonio María Benavides y dale la
corona de tu santa gloria.

TODAS

Amén.

BERNARDA (*Se pone de pie y canta.*)
Requiem aeternam dona eis, Domine.

TODAS (*De pie y cantando al modo gregoriano.*)
Et lux perpetua luceat eis. (*Se santiguan.*)

MUJER 1.ª
Salud para rogar por su alma.

(*Van desfilando.*)

MUJER 3.ª
No te faltará la hogaza de pan caliente.

MUJER 2.ª
Ni el techo para tus hijas.

(*Van desfilando todas por delante de Bernarda y saliendo. Sale Angustias por otra puerta, la que da al patio.*)

MUJER 4.ª
El mismo lujo de tu casamiento lo sigas disfrutando.

PONCIA (*Entrando con una bolsa.*)
De parte de los hombres esta bolsa de dineros para responsos.

BERNARDA
Dales las gracias y échales una copa de aguardiente.

MUCHACHA (*A Magdalena.*)
Magdalena.

BERNARDA
(*A Magdalena, que inicia el llanto.*) Chisss. (*Golpea con el bastón.*) (*Salen todas. A las que se han ido.*) ¡Andar a vuestras cuevas a criticar todo lo que habéis visto! ¡Ojalá tardéis muchos años en pasar el arco de mi puerta!

PONCIA
No tendrás queja ninguna. Ha venido todo el pueblo.

BERNARDA

Sí, para llenar mi casa con el sudor de sus refajos y el veneno de sus lenguas.

AMELIA

¡Madre, no hable usted así!

BERNARDA

Es así como se tiene que hablar en este maldito pueblo sin río, pueblo de pozos, donde siempre se bebe el agua con el miedo de que esté envenenada.

PONCIA

¡Cómo han puesto la solería!

BERNARDA

Igual que si hubiera pasado por ella una manada de cabras. (*La Poncia limpia el suelo.*) Niña, dame un abanico.

ADELA

Tome usted. (*Le da un abanico redondo con flores rojas y verdes.*)

BERNARDA (*Arrojando el abanico al suelo.*)

¿Es éste el abanico que se da a una viuda? Dame uno negro y aprende a respetar el luto de tu padre.

MARTIRIO

Tome usted el mío.

BERNARDA

¿Y tú?

MARTIRIO

Yo no tengo calor.

BERNARDA

Pues busca otro, que te hará falta. En ocho años que dure el luto no ha de entrar en esta casa el viento de la calle. Haceros cuenta que hemos tapiado con ladrillos puertas y ventanas. Así pasó en casa de mi padre y en casa de mi abuelo. Mientras, podéis empezar a bordaros el ajuar. En el arca tengo veinte piezas de hilo

con el que podréis cortar sábanas y embozos. Magdalena puede
bordarlas.

MAGDALENA
Lo mismo me da.[17]

ADELA (*Agria.*)
Si no quieres bordarlas irán sin bordados. Así las tuyas lucirán
más.

MAGDALENA
Ni las mías ni las vuestras. Sé que yo no me voy a casar. Prefiero
llevar sacos al molino. Todo menos estar sentada días y días
dentro de esta sala oscura.

BERNARDA
Eso tiene ser mujer.[18]

MAGDALENA
Malditas sean las mujeres.

BERNARDA
Aquí se hace lo que yo mando. Ya no puedes ir con el cuento a
tu padre. Hilo y aguja para las hembras. Látigo y mula para el
varón. Eso tiene la gente que nace con posibles.[19]

(*Sale Adela.*)

VOZ
Bernarda, ¡déjame salir!

BERNARDA (*En voz alta.*)
¡Dejadla ya!

---

[17] *It's all the same to me.*
[18] *That's a woman's lot.* Note the imposition of sex.
[19] *Needle and thread for females. Whip and mule for the male.
That's the lot of people of substance (born with means).* Note the
imposition of both sex and social position — and the hard imagery
through which the point is made.

(*Sale la Criada.*)

CRIADA

Me ha costado mucho trabajo sujetarla. A pesar de sus ochenta años tu madre es fuerte como un roble.

BERNARDA

Tiene a quien parecérsele. Mi abuela fue igual.[20]

CRIADA

Tuve durante el duelo que taparle varias veces la boca con un costal vacío porque quería llamarte para que le dieras agua de fregar siquiera para beber, y carne de perro, que es lo que ella dice que le das.

MARTIRIO

Tiene mala intención.

BERNARDA (*A la Criada.*)

Déjala que se desahogue en el patio.

CRIADA

Ha sacado del cofre sus anillos y los pendientes de amatistas, se los ha puesto y me ha dicho que se quiere casar.

(*Las hijas ríen.*)

BERNARDA

Ve con ella y ten cuidado que no se acerque al pozo.

CRIADA

No tengas miedo que se tire.

BERNARDA

No es por eso. Pero desde aquel sitio las vecinas pueden verla desde su ventana.

---

[20] *It runs in the family* (lit. *She has someone to take after*). *My grandmother was the same.* Less appropriate *abuelo* in pre-Hernández editions.

(*Sale la Criada.*)

MARTIRIO
Nos vamos a cambiar de ropa.

BERNARDA
Sí, pero no el pañuelo de la cabeza. (*Entra Adela.*) ¿Y Angustias?

ADELA (*Con retintín.*)
La he visto asomada a la rendija del portón. Los hombres se acababan de ir.

BERNARDA
¿Y tú a qué fuiste también al portón?

ADELA
Me llegué a ver si habían puesto las gallinas.

BERNARDA
¡Pero el duelo de los hombres habría salido ya!

ADELA (*Con intención.*)
Todavía estaba un grupo parado por fuera.

BERNARDA (*Furiosa.*)
¡Angustias! ¡Angustias!

ANGUSTIAS (*Entrando.*)
¿Qué manda usted?

BERNARDA
¿Qué mirabas y a quién?

ANGUSTIAS
A nadie.

BERNARDA
¿Es decente que una mujer de tu clase vaya con el anzuelo detrás de un hombre el día de la misa de su padre? ¡Contesta! ¿A quién mirabas?

(*Pausa.*)

ANGUSTIAS
Yo...

BERNARDA
¡Tú!

ANGUSTIAS
¡A nadie!

BERNARDA (*Avanzando con el bastón.*)
¡Suave! ¡Dulzarrona! (*Le da.*)

PONCIA (*Corriendo.*)
¡Bernarda, cálmate! (*La sujeta.*)

(*Angustias llora.*)

BERNARDA
¡Fuera de aquí todas!

(*Salen.*)

PONCIA
Ella lo ha hecho sin dar alcance a lo que hacía, que está francamente mal. ¡Ya me chocó a mí verla escabullirse hacia el patio! Luego estuvo detrás de una ventana oyendo la conversación que traían los hombres, que como siempre no se puede oír.[21]

BERNARDA
¡A eso vienen a los duelos! (*Con curiosidad.*) ¿De qué hablaban?

PONCIA
Hablaban de Paca la Roseta. Anoche ataron a su marido a un pesebre y a ella se la llevaron a la grupa del caballo hasta lo alto del olivar.

BERNARDA
¿Y ella?

---

[21] *listening to the men's talk which, as always, doesn't bear hearing.*

PONCIA

Ella tan conforme. Dicen que iba con los pechos fuera y Maximiliano la llevaba cogida como si tocara la guitarra. ¡Un horror!

BERNARDA

¿Y qué pasó?

PONCIA

Lo que tenía que pasar. Volvieron casi de día. Paca la Roseta traía el pelo suelto y una corona de flores en la cabeza.

BERNARDA

Es la única mujer mala que tenemos en el pueblo.

PONCIA

Porque no es de aquí. Es de muy lejos. Y los que fueron con ella son también hijos de forasteros. Los hombres de aquí no son capaces de eso.

BERNARDA

No, pero les gusta verlo y comentarlo, y se chupan los dedos de que esto ocurra.[22]

PONCIA

Contaban muchas cosas más.

BERNARDA (*Mirando a un lado y otro con cierto temor.*)
¿Cuáles?

PONCIA

Me da vergüenza referirlas.

BERNARDA

Y mi hija las oyó.

PONCIA

¡Claro!

---

[22] *they lick their chops (smack their lips; lit. suck their fingers) that this should happen.*

BERNARDA
Esa sale a sus tías; blancas y untuosas que ponían ojos de carnero al piropo de cualquier barberillo.[23] ¡Cuánto hay que sufrir y luchar para hacer que las personas sean decentes y no tiren al monte demasiado!

PONCIA
¡Es que tus hijas están ya en edad de merecer! Demasiada poca guerra te dan.[24] Angustias ya debe tener mucho más de los treinta.

BERNARDA
Treinta y nueve justos.

PONCIA
Figúrate. Y no ha tenido nunca novio...

BERNARDA (*Furiosa.*)
¡No, no ha tenido novio ninguna, ni les hace falta! Pueden pasarse muy bien.

PONCIA
No he querido ofenderte.

BERNARDA
No hay en cien leguas a la redonda quien se pueda acercar a ellas. Los hombres de aquí no son de su clase. ¿Es que quieres que las entregue a cualquier gañán?

PONCIA
Debías haberte ido a otro pueblo.

BERNARDA
Eso, ¡a venderlas!

---

[23] *She takes after her aunts, that girl; white and sugary and casting sheep's eyes at the flirting of any snippet of a barber.*
[24] *But your daughters are old enough now to look after themselves* (lit. *are now of an age to merit* [*trust, independence, marriage, etc.*]). *They cause you precious little trouble.*

PONCIA

No, Bernarda, a cambiar... ¡Claro que en otros sitios ellas resultan las pobres!

BERNARDA

¡Calla esa lengua atormentadora!

PONCIA

Contigo no se puede hablar. ¿Tenemos o no tenemos confianza?

BERNARDA

No tenemos. Me sirves y te pago. ¡Nada más!

CRIADA (*Entrando.*)

Ahí está don Arturo, que viene a arreglar las particiones.

BERNARDA

Vamos. (*A la Criada.*) Tú empieza a blanquear el patio. (*A Poncia.*) Y tú ve guardando en el arca grande toda la ropa del muerto.

PONCIA

Algunas cosas las podríamos dar...

BERNARDA

Nada. ¡Ni un botón! ¡Ni el pañuelo con que le hemos tapado la cara! (*Sale lentamente apoyada en el bastón y al salir vuelve la cabeza y mira a sus criadas. Las criadas salen después.*)

(*Entran Amelia y Martirio.*)

AMELIA

¿Has tomado la medicina?

MARTIRIO

¡Para lo que me va a servir! [25]

AMELIA

Pero la has tomado.

[25] *For all the good it will do me.*

MARTIRIO

Ya hago las cosas sin fe, pero como un reloj.

AMELIA

Desde que vino el médico nuevo estás más animada.

MARTIRIO

Yo me siento lo mismo.

AMELIA

¿Te fijaste? Adelaida no estuvo en el duelo.

MARTIRIO

Ya lo sabía. Su novio no la deja salir ni al tranco de la calle.
Antes era alegre; ahora ni polvos se echa en la cara.

AMELIA

Ya no sabe una si es mejor tener novio o no.

MARTIRIO

Es lo mismo.

AMELIA

De todo tiene la culpa esta crítica que no nos deja vivir. Adelaida
habrá pasado mal rato.

MARTIRIO

Le tiene miedo a nuestra madre. Es la única que conoce la historia
de su padre y el origen de sus tierras. Siempre que viene le tira
puñaladas con el asunto. Su padre mató en Cuba al marido
de su primera mujer para casarse con ella. Luego, aquí la abandonó
y se fue con otra que tenía una hija, y luego tuvo relaciones con
esta muchacha, la madre de Adelaida, y se casó con ella después
de haber muerto loca la segunda mujer.

AMELIA

Y ese infame, ¿por qué no está en la cárcel?

MARTIRIO

Porque los hombres se tapan unos a otros las cosas de esta índole
y nadie es capaz de delatar.

AMELIA

Pero Adelaida no tiene culpa de esto.

MARTIRIO

No, pero las cosas se repiten. Yo veo que todo es una terrible
repetición. Y ella tiene el mismo sino de su madre y de su abuela,
mujeres las dos del que la engendró.

AMELIA

¡Qué cosa más grande! [26]

MARTIRIO

Es preferible no ver a un hombre nunca. Desde niña les tuve
miedo. Los veía en el corral uncir los bueyes y levantar los
costales de trigo entre voces y zapatazos, y siempre tuve miedo
de crecer por temor de encontrarme de pronto abrazada por
ellos. Dios me ha hecho débil y fea y los ha apartado definitivamente de mí.

AMELIA

¡Eso no digas! Enrique Humanes estuvo detrás de ti y le gusta-
bas.[27]

MARTIRIO

¡Invenciones de la gente! Una vez estuve en camisa detrás de la
ventana hasta que fue de día, porque me avisó con la hija de su
gañán que iba a venir, y no vino. Fue todo cosa de lenguas.[28]
Luego se casó con otra que tenía más que yo.

AMELIA

¡Y fea como un demonio!

MARTIRIO

¡Qué les importa a ellos la fealdad! A ellos les importa la tierra,
las yuntas y una perra sumisa que les dé de comer.

---

[26] *What a terrible thing!*
[27] Endnote F.
[28] *It was all just talk.*

AMELIA
  ¡Ay!

(*Entra Magdalena.*)

MAGDALENA
  ¿Qué hacéis?

MARTIRIO
  Aquí.[29]

AMELIA
  ¿Y tú?

MAGDALENA
  Vengo de correr las cámaras. Por andar un poco. De ver los
  cuadros bordados en cañamazo de nuestra abuela, el perrito
  de lanas y el negro luchando con el león, que tanto nos gustaba
  de niñas. Aquélla era una época más alegre. Una boda duraba
  diez días y no se usaban las malas lenguas.[30] Hoy hay más finura.
  Las novias se ponen velo blanco como en las poblaciones, y se
  bebe vino de botella, pero nos pudrimos por el qué dirán.

MARTIRIO
  ¡Sabe Dios lo que entonces pasaría!

AMELIA (*A Magdalena.*)
  Llevas desabrochados los cordones de un zapato.

MAGDALENA
  ¡Qué más da! [31]

AMELIA
  ¡Te los vas a pisar y te vas a caer!

---

[29] i.e. *Aquí estamos. Aquí nos tienes.* Common replies to indicate
Nothing special, Just messing about, Just chatting, etc.

[30] *people didn't speak ill of one another.* Note the emphasis on
gossip (cf. *cosa de lenguas, el qué dirán* [lit. *what people will say*], *esta
crítica que no nos deja vivir*, etc.).

[31] *What does it matter?*

MAGDALENA
¡Una menos!

MARTIRIO
¿Y Adela?

MAGDALENA
¡Ah! Se ha puesto el traje verde que se hizo para estrenar el día de su cumpleaños, se ha ido al corral y ha comenzado a voces: '¡Gallinas, gallinas, miradme!' ¡Me he tenido que reír!

AMELIA
¡Si la hubiera visto madre!

MAGDALENA
¡Pobrecilla! Es la más joven de nosotras y tiene ilusión. ¡Daría algo por verla feliz!

(*Pausa. Angustias cruza la escena con unas toallas en la mano.*)

ANGUSTIAS
¿Qué hora es?

MARTIRIO
Ya deben ser las doce.

ANGUSTIAS
¿Tanto?

AMELIA
Estarán al caer.

(*Sale Angustias.*)

MAGDALENA (*Con intención.*)
¿Sabéis ya la cosa?... (*Señalando a Angustias.*)

AMELIA
No.

MAGDALENA
¡Vamos!

MARTIRIO

¡No sé a qué cosa te refieres!...

MAGDALENA

Mejor que yo lo sabéis las dos, siempre cabeza con cabeza como
dos ovejitas, pero sin desahogaros con nadie. ¡Lo de Pepe el
Romano!

MARTIRIO

¡Ah!

MAGDALENA (*Remedándola.*)

¡Ah! Ya se comenta por el pueblo. Pepe el Romano viene a
casarse con Angustias. Anoche estuvo rondando la casa y creo
que pronto va a mandar un emisario.

MARTIRIO

¡Yo me alegro! Es buen hombre.

AMELIA

Yo también. Angustias tiene buenas condiciones.

MAGDALENA

Ninguna de las dos os alegráis.

MARTIRIO

¡Magdalena! ¡Mujer!

MAGDALENA

Si viniera por el tipo de Angustias, por Angustias como mujer,
yo me alegraría; pero viene por el dinero. Aunque Angustias es
nuestra hermana, aquí estamos en familia y reconocemos que
está vieja, enfermiza, y que siempre ha sido la que ha tenido
menos mérito de todas nosotras. Porque si con veinte años
parecía un palo vestido, ¡qué será ahora que tiene cuarenta!

MARTIRIO

No hables así. La suerte viene a quien menos la aguarda.

AMELIA

¡Después de todo dice la verdad! Angustias tiene el dinero de

su padre, es la única rica de la casa y por eso, ahora que nuestro
padre ha muerto y ya se harán particiones, vienen por ella.

MAGDALENA

Pepe el Romano tiene veinticinco años y es el mejor tipo de todos
estos contornos.[32] Lo natural sería que te pretendiera a ti,
Amelia, o a nuestra Adela, que tiene veinte años, pero no que
venga a buscar lo más oscuro de esta casa, a una mujer que como
su padre habla con la nariz.[33]

MARTIRIO

¡Puede que a él le guste!

MAGDALENA

¡Nunca he podido resistir tu hipocresía!

MARTIRIO

¡Dios nos valga! [34]

(Entra Adela.)

MAGDALENA

¿Te han visto ya las gallinas?

ADELA

¿Y qué querías que hiciera?

AMELIA

¡Si te ve nuestra madre te arrastra del pelo!

ADELA

Tenía mucha ilusión con el vestido. Pensaba ponérmelo el día que
vamos a comer sandías a la noria. No hubiera habido otro igual.

MARTIRIO

¡Es un vestido precioso!

---

[32] the best-looking lad for miles around.
[33] through her nose.
[34] Heaven preserve us!

ADELA

Y me está muy bien. Es lo que mejor ha cortado Magdalena.

MAGDALENA

Y las gallinas, ¿qué te han dicho?

ADELA

Regalarme unas cuantas pulgas que me han acribillado las piernas.

(*Ríen.*)

MARTIRIO

Lo que puedes hacer es teñirlo de negro.

MAGDALENA

¡Lo mejor que puede hacer es regalárselo a Angustias para su boda con Pepe el Romano!

ADELA (*Con emoción contenida.*)

Pero Pepe el Romano...

AMELIA

¿No lo has oído decir?

ADELA

No.

MAGDALENA

¡Pues ya lo sabes!

ADELA

¡Pero si no puede ser!

MAGDALENA

¡El dinero lo puede todo!

ADELA

¿Por eso ha salido detrás del duelo y estuvo mirando por el portón? (*Pausa.*) Y ese hombre es capaz de...

MAGDALENA

Es capaz de todo.

(*Pausa.*)

MARTIRIO
¿Qué piensas, Adela?

ADELA
Pienso que este luto me ha cogido en la peor época de mi vida para pasarlo.

MAGDALENA
Ya te acostumbrarás.

ADELA (*Rompiendo a llorar con ira.*)
¡No, no me acostumbraré! Yo no quiero estar encerrada. No quiero que se me pongan las carnes como a vosotras.[35] ¡No quiero perder mi blancura en estas habitaciones! ¡Mañana me pondré mi vestido verde y me echaré a pasear por la calle! ¡Yo quiero salir!

(*Entra la Criada.*)

MAGDALENA (*Autoritaria.*)
¡Adela!

CRIADA
¡La pobre! ¡Cuánto ha sentido a su padre! (*Sale.*)

MARTIRIO
¡Calla!

AMELIA
Lo que sea de una será de todas.

(*Adela se calma.*)

MAGDALENA
Ha estado a punto de oírte la criada.

CRIADA (*Apareciendo.*)
Pepe el Romano viene por lo alto de la calle.

---

[35] *I don't want my flesh to turn like yours.*

(*Amelia, Martirio y Magdalena corren presurosas.*)

MAGDALENA
¡Vamos a verlo!

(*Salen rápidas.*)

CRIADA (*A Adela.*)
¿Tú no vas?

ADELA
No me importa.

CRIADA
Como dará la vuelta a la esquina, desde la ventana de tu cuarto
se verá mejor. (*Sale la Criada.*)

(*Adela queda en escena dudando. Después de un instante se va
también rápida hacia su habitación. Salen Bernarda y la Poncia.*)

BERNARDA
¡Malditas particiones!

PONCIA
¡ ¡Cuánto dinero le queda a Angustias! !

BERNARDA
Sí.

PONCIA
Y a las otras bastante menos.

BERNARDA
Ya me lo has dicho tres veces y no te he querido replicar. Bastante
menos, mucho menos. No me lo recuerdes más.

(*Sale Angustias muy compuesta de cara.*)

BERNARDA
¡Angustias!

ANGUSTIAS
Madre.

BERNARDA

¿Pero has tenido valor de echarte polvos en la cara? ¿Has tenido valor de lavarte la cara el día de la misa de tu padre?

ANGUSTIAS

No era mi padre. El mío murió hace tiempo. ¿Es que ya no lo recuerda usted?

BERNARDA

¡Más debes a este hombre, padre de tus hermanas, que al tuyo! Gracias a este hombre tienes colmada tu fortuna.

ANGUSTIAS

¡Eso lo teníamos que ver! [36]

BERNARDA

¡Aunque fuera por decencia! Por respeto.

ANGUSTIAS

Madre, déjeme usted salir.

BERNARDA

¿Salir? Después que te haya quitado esos polvos de la cara. ¡Suavona! ¡Yeyo! [37] ¡Espejo de tus tías (*Le quita violentamente con su pañuelo los polvos.*) ¡Ahora vete!

PONCIA

¡Bernarda, no seas tan inquisitiva!

BERNARDA

Aunque mi madre esté loca yo estoy con mis cinco sentidos y sé perfectamente lo que hago.

(*Entran todas.*)

MAGDALENA

¿Qué pasa?

---

[36] *That remains to be seen.*
[37] *Two-faced creature! Painted (Brazen) hussy!*

BERNARDA
No pasa nada.

MAGDALENA (*A Angustias.*)
Si es que discutís por las particiones, tú, que eres la más rica, te puedes quedar con todo.

ANGUSTIAS
¡Guárdate la lengua en la madriguera!

BERNARDA (*Golpeando con el bastón en el suelo.*)
¡No os hagáis ilusiones de que vais a poder conmigo! ¡Hasta que salga de esta casa con los pies delante mandaré en lo mío y en lo vuestro! [38]

(*Se oyen unas voces y entra en escena María Josefa, la madre de Bernarda, viejísima, ataviada con flores en la cabeza y en el pecho.*)

MARÍA JOSEFA
Bernarda, ¿dónde está mí mantilla? Nada de lo que tengo quiero que sea para vosotras. Ni mis anillos, ni mi traje negro de moaré. Porque ninguna de vosotras se va a casar. ¡Ninguna! ¡Bernarda, dame mi gargantilla de perlas!

BERNARDA (*A la Criada.*)
¿Por qué la habéis dejado entrar?

CRIADA (*Temblando.*)
¡Se me escapó!

MARÍA JOSEFA
Me escapé porque me quiero casar, porque quiero casarme con un varón hermoso de la orilla del mar, ya que aquí los hombres huyen de las mujeres.

BERNARDA
¡Calle usted, madre!

---

[38] *Don't kid yourselves you can get the better of me. Until I leave this house feet first I'll be in charge in my affairs and in yours.*

MARÍA JOSEFA

No, no callo. No quiero ver a estas mujeres solteras, rabiando por la boda, haciéndose polvo el corazón,[39] y yo me quiero ir a mi pueblo. ¡Bernarda, yo quiero un varón para casarme y tener alegría!

BERNARDA

¡Encerradla!

MARÍA JOSEFA

¡Déjame salir, Bernarda!

(*La Criada coge a María Josefa.*)

BERNARDA

¡Ayudarla vosotras!

(*Todas arrastran a la vieja.*)

MARÍA JOSEFA

¡Quiero irme de aquí! ¡Bernarda! ¡A casarme a la orilla del mar, a la orilla del mar!

TELON RAPIDO

---

[39] *I don't want to see these spinster women craving for marriage, eating their hearts out.*

ACTO SEGUNDO[1]

Habitación blanca del interior de la casa de Bernarda. Las puertas de la izquierda dan a los dormitorios. Las hijas de Bernarda están sentadas en sillas bajas, cosiendo. Magdalena borda. Con ellas está la Poncia.

ANGUSTIAS
Ya he cortado la tercera sábana.

MARTIRIO
Le corresponde a Amelia.

MAGDALENA
Angustias, ¿pongo también las iniciales de Pepe?

ANGUSTIAS (*Seca.*)
No.

MAGDALENA (*A voces.*)
Adela, ¿no vienes?

AMELIA
Estará echada en la cama.

PONCIA
Esa tiene algo. La encuentro sin sosiego, temblona, asustada como si tuviera una lagartija entre los pechos.[2]

---

[1] Introduction, p. xi.
[2] *There's something wrong with that girl. I find her restless, trembly, frightened as though she had a lizard between her breasts.*

MARTIRIO

No tiene ni más ni menos que lo que tenemos todas.

MAGDALENA

Todas menos Angustias.

ANGUSTIAS

Yo me encuentro bien, y al que le duela que reviente.[3]

MAGDALENA

Desde luego hay que reconocer que lo mejor que has tenido siempre ha sido el talle y la delicadeza.

ANGUSTIAS

Afortunadamente pronto voy a salir de este infierno.

MAGDALENA

¡A lo mejor no sales!

MARTIRIO

¡Dejar esa conversación!

ANGUSTIAS

Y, además, ¡más vale onza en el arca que ojos negros en la cara![4]

MAGDALENA

Por un oído me entra y por otro me sale.

AMELIA (*A la Poncia.*)

Abre la puerta del patio a ver si nos entra un poco el fresco. (*La Poncia lo hace.*)

MARTIRIO

Esta noche pasada no me podía quedar dormida del calor.

AMELIA

¡Yo tampoco!

---

[3] *I'm all right, and to hell with anyone who doesn't like it* (lit. *anyone who grieves over it, may he burst*).

[4] *Besides, better to have gold in your coffers than dark (pretty) eyes in your face.*

MAGDALENA

Yo me levanté a refrescarme. Había un nublo negro de tormenta y hasta cayeron algunas gotas.[5]

PONCIA

Era la una de la madrugada y salía fuego de la tierra. También me levanté yo. Todavía estaba Angustias con Pepe en la ventana.

MAGDALENA (*Con ironía.*)

¿Tan tarde? ¿A qué hora se fue?

ANGUSTIAS

Magdalena, ¿a qué preguntas si lo viste?

AMELIA

Se iría a eso de la una y media.

ANGUSTIAS

Sí. ¿Tú por qué lo sabes?

AMELIA

Lo sentí toser y oí los pasos de su jaca.

PONCIA

¡Pero si yo lo sentí marchar a eso de las cuatro!

ANGUSTIAS

¡No sería él!

PONCIA

¡Estoy segura!

MARTIRIO

A mí también me pareció.

MAGDALENA

¡Qué cosa más rara!

(*Pausa.*)

---

[5] *There was a black storm cloud and we even had a few drops of rain.*

PONCIA

Oye, Angustias, ¿qué fue lo que te dijo la primera vez que se acercó a tu ventana?

ANGUSTIAS

Nada. ¡Qué me iba a decir! Cosas de conversación.

MARTIRIO

Verdaderamente es raro que dos personas que no se conocen se vean de pronto en una reja y ya novios.

ANGUSTIAS

Pues a mí no me chocó.

AMELIA

A mí me daría no sé qué.[6]

ANGUSTIAS

No, porque cuando un hombre se acerca a una reja ya sabe por los que van y vienen, llevan y traen, que se le va a decir que sí.

MARTIRIO

Bueno, pero él te lo tendría que decir.

ANGUSTIAS

¡Claro!

AMELIA (*Curiosa.*)

¿Y cómo te lo dijo?

ANGUSTIAS

Pues, nada: 'Ya sabes que ando detrás de ti, necesito una mujer buena, modosa, y ésa eres tú si me das la conformidad.'

AMELIA

¡A mí me da vergüenza de estas cosas!

ANGUSTIAS

¡Y a mí, pero hay que pasarlas!

---

[6] *I'd feel a bit queer about it.*

PONCIA
    ¿Y habló más?

ANGUSTIAS
    Sí, siempre habló él.

MARTIRIO
    ¿Y tú?

ANGUSTIAS
    Yo no hubiera podido. Casi se me salía el corazón por la boca.
    Era la primera vez que estaba sola de noche con un hombre.

MAGDALENA
    Y un hombre tan guapo.

ANGUSTIAS
    ¡No tiene mal tipo! [7]

PONCIA
    Esas cosas pasan entre personas ya un poco instruidas que hablan
    y dicen y mueven la mano... La primera vez que mi marido
    Evaristo el Colorín vino a mi ventana...[8] ¡Ja, ja ja!

AMELIA
    ¿Qué pasó?

PONCIA
    Era muy oscuro. Lo vi acercarse y, al llegar, me dijo: 'Buenas
    noches.' 'Buenas noches', le dije yo, y nos quedamos callados
    más de media hora. Me corría el sudor por todo el cuerpo. En-
    tonces Evaristo se acercó, se acercó que se quería meter por los
    hierros, y dijo con voz muy baja: '¡Ven, que te tiente!'[9]

(*Ríen todas. Amelia se levanta corriendo y espía por una puerta.*)

AMELIA
    ¡Ay! Creí que llegaba nuestra madre.

> [7] *He's not bad-looking.*
> [8] Evaristo el Colín in pre-Hernández editions.
> [9] *'Come and let me feel you!'*

MAGDALENA

¡Buenas nos hubiera puesto! [10]

(*Siguen riendo.*)

AMELIA

Chiss... ¡Que nos va a oír!

PONCIA

Luego se portó bien. En vez de darle por otra cosa, le dio por criar colorines hasta que murió.[11] A vosotras, que sois solteras, os conviene saber de todos modos que el hombre a los quince días de boda deja la cama por la mesa, y luego la mesa por la tabernilla. Y la que no se conforma se pudre llorando en un rincón.

AMELIA

Tú te conformaste.

PONCIA

¡Yo pude con él!

MARTIRIO

¿Es verdad que le pegaste algunas veces?

PONCIA

Sí, y por poco lo dejo tuerto.[12]

MAGDALENA

¡Así debían ser todas las mujeres!

PONCIA

Yo tengo la escuela de tu madre. Un día me dijo no sé qué cosa y le maté todos los colorines con la mano del almirez.

(*Ríen.*)

---

[10] *We wouldn't half have been in for it.*

[11] *Instead of taking to other things, he took to breeding linnets until he died.*

[12] *I very nearly poked his eye out* (lit. *I all but leave him one-eyed*).

MAGDALENA
Adela, niña, no te pierdas esto.

AMELIA
Adela.

(*Pausa.*)

MAGDALENA
¡Voy a ver! (*Entra.*)

PONCIA
¡Esa niña está mala!

MARTIRIO
Claro, ¡no duerme apenas!

PONCIA
Pues, ¿qué hace?

MARTIRIO
¡Yo qué sé lo que hace!

PONCIA
Mejor lo sabrás tú que yo, que duermes pared por medio.[13]

ANGUSTIAS
La envidia la come.

AMELIA
No exageres.

ANGUSTIAS
Se lo noto en los ojos. Se le está poniendo mirar de loca.

MARTIRIO
No habléis de locos. Aquí es el único sitio donde no se puede pronunciar esta palabra.

(*Sale Magdalena con Adela.*)

[13] *in the next room* (lit. [*with only a*] *wall between*).

MAGDALENA
   Pues, ¿no estabas dormida?

ADELA
   Tengo mal cuerpo.[14]

MARTIRIO (*Con intención.*)
   ¿Es que no has dormido bien esta noche?

ADELA
   Sí.

MARTIRIO
   ¿Entonces?

ADELA (*Fuerte.*)
   ¡Déjame ya! ¡Durmiendo o velando, no tienes por qué meterte
en lo mío! [15] ¡Yo hago con mi cuerpo lo que me parece!

MARTIRIO
   ¡Sólo es interés por ti!

ADELA
   Interés o inquisición. ¿No estabais cosiendo? Pues seguir. ¡Quisiera ser invisible, pasar por las habitaciones sin que me pregun-
tarais dónde voy!

CRIADA (*Entra.*)
   Bernarda os llama. Está el hombre de los encajes.

   (*Salen. Al salir, Martirio mira fijamente a Adela.*)

ADELA
   ¡No me mires más! Si quieres te daré mis ojos, que son frescos,
y mis espaldas, para que te compongas la joroba que tienes, pero
vuelve la cabeza cuando yo pase.

   (*Se va Martirio.*)

---

[14] *I don't feel well.*
[15] *Sleeping or waking, you've no reason to meddle in my affairs.*

PONCIA

¡Adela, que es tu hermana, y además la que más te quiere!

ADELA

Me sigue a todos lados. A veces se asoma a mi cuarto para ver si duermo. No me deja respirar. Y siempre: '¡Qué lástima de cara! ¡Qué lástima de cuerpo, que no va a ser para nadie! ' ¡Y eso no! ¡Mi cuerpo será de quien yo quiera!

PONCIA (*Con intención y en voz baja.*)

De Pepe el Romano, ¿no es eso?

ADELA (*Sobrecogida.*)

¿Qué dices?

PONCIA

¡Lo que digo, Adela!

ADELA

¡Calla!

PONCIA (*Alto.*)

¿Crees que no me he fijado?

ADELA

¡Baja la voz!

PONCIA

¡Mata esos pensamientos!

ADELA

¿Qué sabes tú?

PONCIA

Las viejas vemos a través de las paredes. ¿Dónde vas de noche cuando te levantas?

ADELA

¡Ciega debías estar!

PONCIA

Con la cabeza y las manos llenas de ojos cuando se trata de lo

que se trata. Por mucho que pienso no sé lo que te propones.
¿Por qué te pusiste casi desnuda con la luz encendida y la ventana
abierta al pasar Pepe el segundo día que vino a hablar con tu
hermana?

ADELA

¡Eso no es verdad!

PONCIA

¡No seas como los niños chicos! Deja en paz a tu hermana, y
si Pepe el Romano te gusta te aguantas. (*Adela llora.*) Además
¿quién dice que no te puedas casar con él? Tu hermana Angustias
es una enferma. Esa no resiste el primer parto. Es estrecha de
cintura, vieja, y con mi conocimiento te digo que se morirá.
Entonces Pepe hará lo que hacen todos los viudos de esta tierra:
se casará con la más joven, la más hermosa, y ésa eres tú. Ali-
menta esa esperanza, olvídalo. Lo que quieras, pero no vayas
contra la ley de Dios.

ADELA

¡Calla!

PONCIA

¡No callo!

ADELA

Métete en tus cosas. ¡Oledora! ¡Pérfida! [16]

PONCIA

¡Sombra tuya he de ser!

ADELA

En vez de limpiar la casa y acostarte para rezar a tus muertos,
buscas como una vieja marrana asuntos de hombres y mujeres
para babosear en ellos.

PONCIA

¡Velo!, para que las gentes no escupan al pasar por esta puerta.

---

[16] *Mind your own business. Snooper! Traitor!*

ADELA

¡Qué cariño tan grande te ha entrado de pronto por mi hermana!

PONCIA

No os tengo ley a ninguna, pero quiero vivir en casa decente. ¡No quiero mancharme de vieja!

ADELA

Es inútil tu consejo. Ya es tarde. No por encima de ti, que eres una criada; por encima de mi madre saltaría para apagarme este fuego que tengo levantado por piernas y boca. ¿Qué puedes decir de mí? ¿Que me encierro en mi cuarto y no abro la puerta? ¿Que no duermo? ¡Soy más lista que tú! Mira a ver si puedes agarrar la liebre con tus manos.[17]

PONCIA

No me desafíes. ¡Adela, no me desafíes! Porque yo puedo dar voces, encender luces y hacer que toquen las campanas.

ADELA

Trae cuatro mil bengalas amarillas y ponlas en las bardas del corral. Nadie podrá evitar que suceda lo que tiene que suceder.

PONCIA

¡Tanto te gusta ese hombre!

ADELA

¡Tanto! Mirando sus ojos me parece que bebo su sangre lentamente.

PONCIA

Yo no te puedo oír.

ADELA

¡Pues me oirás! Te he tenido miedo. ¡Pero ya soy más fuerte que tú!

(*Entra Angustias.*)

---

[17] *See if you can catch the hare with your hands.*

ANGUSTIAS
   ¡Siempre discutiendo!

PONCIA
   Claro, se empeña en que, con el calor que hace, vaya a traerle
   no sé qué cosa de la tienda.

ANGUSTIAS
   ¿Me compraste el bote de esencia?

PONCIA
   El más caro. Y los polvos. En la mesa de tu cuarto los he puesto.

   (*Sale Angustias.*)

ADELA
   ¡Y chitón!

PONCIA
   ¡Lo veremos!

   (*Entran Martirio, Amelia y Magdalena.*)

MAGDALENA (*A Adela.*)
   ¿Has visto los encajes?

AMELIA
   Los de Angustias para sus sábanas de novia son preciosos.

ADELA (*A Martirio, que trae unos encajes.*)
   ¿Y éstos?

MARTIRIO
   Son para mí. Para una camisa.

ADELA (*Con sarcasmo.*)
   ¡Se necesita buen humor!

MARTIRIO (*Con intención.*)
   Para verlos yo. No necesito lucirme ante nadie.

PONCIA
   Nadie la ve a una en camisa.

MARTIRIO (*Con intención y mirando a Adela.*)

¡A veces! Pero me encanta la ropa interior. Si fuera rica la tendría de holanda. Es uno de los pocos gustos que me quedan.

PONCIA

Estos encajes son preciosos para las gorras de niño, para mantehuelos de cristianar. Yo nunca pude usarlos en los míos. A ver si ahora Angustias los usa en los suyos. Como le dé por tener crías vais a estar cosiendo mañana y tarde.[18]

MAGDALENA

Yo no pienso dar una puntada.

AMELIA

Y mucho menos cuidar niños ajenos. Mira tú cómo están las vecinas del callejón, sacrificadas por cuatro monigotes.

PONCIA

Esas están mejor que vosotras. ¡Siquiera allí se ríe y se oyen porrazos!

MARTIRIO

Pues vete a servir con ellas.

PONCIA

No. Ya me ha tocado en suerte este convento.[19]

(*Se oyen unos campanillos lejanos como a través de varios muros.*)

MAGDALENA

Son los hombres que vuelven al trabajo.

PONCIA

Hace un minuto dieron las tres.

MARTIRIO

¡Con este sol!

---

[18] *If she takes to having babies (children) you'll be sewing all day long (morning, noon and night).*

[19] *I'm landed with this convent.*

ADELA (*Sentándose.*)
   ¡Ay, quién pudiera salir también a los campos!

MAGDALENA (*Sentándose.*)
   ¡Cada clase tiene que hacer lo suyo!

MARTIRIO (*Sentándose.*)
   ¡Así es!

AMELIA (*Sentándose.*)
   ¡Ay!

PONCIA
   No hay alegría como la de los campos en esta época. Ayer de
   mañana llegaron los segadores. Cuarenta o cincuenta buenos
   mozos.

MAGDALENA
   ¿De dónde son este año?

PONCIA
   De muy lejos. Vinieron de los montes. ¡Alegres! ¡Como árboles
   quemados! ¡Dando voces y arrojando piedras! Anoche llegó
   al pueblo una mujer vestida de lentejuelas y que bailaba con un
   acordeón, y quince de ellos la contrataron para llevársela al
   olivar. Yo los vi de lejos. El que la contrataba era un muchacho
   de ojos verdes, apretado como una gavilla de trigo.

AMELIA
   ¿Es eso cierto?

ADELA
   ¡Pero es posible!

PONCIA
   Hace años vino otra de éstas y yo misma di dinero a mi hijo
   mayor para que fuera. Los hombres necesitan estas cosas.

ADELA
   Se les perdona todo.

AMELIA

Nacer mujer es el mayor castigo.

MAGDALENA

Y ni nuestros ojos siquiera nos pertenecen.

(*Se oye un cantar lejano que se va acercando.*)

PONCIA

Son ellos. Traen unos cantos preciosos.

AMELIA

Ahora salen a segar.

CORO

> Ya salen los segadores
> en busca de las espigas;
> se llevan los corazones
> de las muchachas que miran.

(*Se oyen panderos y carrañacas. Pausa. Todas oyen en un silencio traspasado por el sol.*)

AMELIA

¡Y no les importa el calor!

MARTIRIO

Siegan entre llamaradas.

ADELA

Me gustaría segar para ir y venir. Así se olvida lo que nos muerde.

MARTIRIO

¿Qué tienes tú que olvidar?

ADELA

Cada una sabe sus cosas.

MARTIRIO (*Profunda.*)

¡Cada una!

PONCIA

¡Callar! ¡Callar!

CORO (*Muy lejano.*)
>   Abrir puertas y ventanas
> las que vivís en el pueblo;
> el segador pide rosas
> para adornar su sombrero.

PONCIA
  ¡Qué canto!

MARTIRIO (*Con nostalgia.*)
>   Abrir puertas y ventanas
> las que vivís en el pueblo...

ADELA (*Con pasión.*)
>   ... el segador pide rosas
> para adornar su sombrero.

  (*Se va alejando el cantar.*)

PONCIA
  Ahora dan la vuelta a la esquina.

ADELA
  Vamos a verlos por la ventana de mi cuarto.

PONCIA
  Tened cuidado con no entreabrirla mucho, porque son capaces de dar un empujón para ver quién mira.

  (*Se van las tres. Martirio queda sentada en la silla baja con la cabeza entre las manos.*)

AMELIA (*Acercándose.*)
  ¿Qué te pasa?

MARTIRIO
  Me sienta mal el calor.

AMELIA
  ¿No es más que eso?

MARTIRIO
Estoy deseando que llegue noviembre, los días de lluvia, la escarcha; todo lo que no sea este verano interminable.

AMELIA
Ya pasará y volverá otra vez.

MARTIRIO
¡Claro! (*Pausa.*) ¿A qué hora te dormiste anoche?

AMELIA
No sé. Yo duermo como un tronco. ¿Por qué?

MARTIRIO
Por nada, pero me pareció oír gente en el corral.

AMELIA
¿Sí?

MARTIRIO
Muy tarde.

AMELIA
¿Y no tuviste miedo?

MARTIRIO
No. Ya lo he oído otras noches.

AMELIA
Debíamos tener cuidado. ¿No serían los gañanes?

MARTIRIO
Los gañanes llegan a las seis.

AMELIA
Quizá una mulilla sin desbravar.

MARTIRIO (*Entre dientes y llena de segunda intención.*)
Eso, ¡eso!, una mulilla sin desbravar.

AMELIA
¡Hay que prevenir!

MARTIRIO
  ¡No, no! No digas nada. Puede ser un barrunto mío.

AMELIA
  Quizá.

  (*Pausa. Amelia inicia el mutis.*)

MARTIRIO
  Amelia.

AMELIA (*En la puerta.*)
  ¿Qué?

  (*Pausa.*)

MARTIRIO
  Nada.

  (*Pausa.*)

AMELIA
  ¿Por qué me llamaste?

  (*Pausa.*)

MARTIRIO
  Se me escapó. Fue sin darme cuenta.

  (*Pausa.*)

AMELIA
  Acuéstate un poco.

ANGUSTIAS (*Entrando furiosa en escena, de modo que haya un gran contraste con los silencios anteriores.*)
  ¿Dónde está el retrato de Pepe que tenía yo debajo de mi almohada? ¿Quién de vosotras lo tiene?

MARTIRIO
  Ninguna.

AMELIA
   Ni que Pepe fuera un San Bartolomé de plata.[20]

   (*Entran Poncia, Magdalena y Adela.*)

ANGUSTIAS
   ¿Dónde está el retrato?

ADELA
   ¿Qué retrato?

ANGUSTIAS
   Una de vosotras me lo ha escondido.

MAGDALENA
   ¿Tienes la desvergüenza de decir esto?

ANGUSTIAS
   Estaba en mi cuarto y ya no está.

MARTIRIO
   ¿Y no se habrá escapado a medianoche al corral? A Pepe le
gusta andar con la luna.

ANGUSTIAS
   ¡No me gastes bromas! Cuando venga se lo contaré.

PONCIA
   ¡Eso, no! ¡Porque aparecerá! (*Mirando a Adela.*)

ANGUSTIAS
   ¡Me gustaría saber cuál de vosotras lo tiene!

ADELA (*Mirando a Martirio.*)
   ¡Alguna! ¡Todas menos yo!

MARTIRIO (*Con intención.*)
   ¡Desde luego!

----

[20] *Not even if Pepe were a Saint Bartholomew of silver.* In Andalusia
Saint Bartholomew (like Saint Luis) is associated with good looks.

BERNARDA (*Entrando con su bastón.*)
¡Qué escándalo es éste en mi casa y con el silencio del peso del calor! Estarán las vecinas con el oído pegado a los tabiques.

ANGUSTIAS
Me han quitado el retrato de mi novio.

BERNARDA (*Fiera.*)
¿Quién? ¿Quién?

ANGUSTIAS
¡Estas!

BERNARDA
¿Cuál de vosotras? (*Silencio.*) ¡Contestarme! (*Silencio. A Poncia.*) Registra los cuartos, mira por las camas. Esto tiene no ataros más cortas. ¡Pero me vais a soñar! [21] (*A Angustias.*) ¿Estás segura?

ANGUSTIAS
Sí.

BERNARDA
¿Lo has buscado bien?

ANGUSTIAS
Sí, madre.

(*Todas están de pie en medio de un embarazoso silencio.*)

BERNARDA
Me hacéis al final de mi vida beber el veneno más amargo que una madre puede resistir. (*A Poncia.*) ¿No lo encuentras?

(*Sale Poncia.*)

PONCIA
Aquí está.

---

[21] *This comes of not keeping you on a shorter lead. But I'll see you regret it* (i.e. you'll [have reason to] dream of me [and the torments I'll make you suffer]).

BERNARDA
¿Dónde lo has encontrado?

PONCIA
Estaba...

BERNARDA
Dilo sin temor.

PONCIA (*Extrañada.*)
Entre las sábanas de la cama de Martirio.

BERNARDA (*A Martirio.*)
¿Es verdad?

MARTIRIO
¡Es verdad!

BERNARDA (*Avanzando y golpeándola con el bastón.*)
¡Mala puñalada te den, mosca muerta! ¡Sembradura de vidrios! [22]

MARTIRIO (*Fiera.*)
¡No me pegue usted, madre!

BERNARDA
¡Todo lo que quiera!

MARTIRIO
¡Si yo la dejo! ¿Lo oye? ¡Retírese usted!

PONCIA
No faltes a tu madre.

ANGUSTIAS (*Cogiendo a Bernarda.*)
Déjela. ¡Por favor!

BERNARDA
Ni lágrimas te quedan en esos ojos.

---

[22] *Damn your eyes* (lit. *May they give you a bad dagger stroke*), *you two-faced wretch! Sower of discord!* (lit. *pieces of glass*).

MARTIRIO

No voy a llorar para darle gusto.

BERNARDA

¿Por qué has cogido el retrato?

MARTIRIO

¿Es que yo no puedo gastar una broma a mi hermana? ¿Para qué otra cosa lo iba a querer?

ADELA (*Saltando llena de celos.*)[23]

No ha sido broma, que tú no has gustado jamás de juegos. Ha sido otra cosa que te reventaba en el pecho por querer salir. Dilo ya claramente.

MARTIRIO

¡Calla y no me hagas hablar, que si hablo se van a juntar las paredes unas con otras de vergüenza!

ADELA

¡La mala lengua no tiene fin para inventar! [24]

BERNARDA

¡Adela!

MAGDALENA

Estáis locas.

AMELIA

Y nos apedreáis con malos pensamientos.

MARTIRIO

Otras hacen cosas más malas.

ADELA

Hasta que se pongan en cueros de una vez y se las lleve el río.[25]

---

[23] *Exploding with jealousy.*
[24] *There's no end to the inventions of an evil tongue.*
[25] *Until they finally strip naked and are swept away by the river.*

BERNARDA
¡Perversa!

ANGUSTIAS
Yo no tengo la culpa de que Pepe el Romano se haya fijado en mí.

ADELA
¡Por tus dineros!

ANGUSTIAS
¡Madre!

BERNARDA
¡Silencio!

MARTIRIO
Por tus marjales y tus arboledas.

MAGDALENA
¡Eso es lo justo!

BERNARDA
¡Silencio digo! Yo veía la tormenta venir, pero no creía que estallara tan pronto. ¡Ay, qué pedrisco de odio habéis echado sobre mi corazón! Pero todavía no soy anciana y tengo cinco cadenas para vosotras y esta casa levantada por mi padre para que ni las hierbas se enteren de mi desolación. ¡Fuera de aquí! (*Salen. Bernarda se sienta desolada. Poncia está de pie arrimada a los muros. Bernarda reacciona, da un golpe en el suelo y dice:*) ¡Tendré que sentarles la mano! Bernarda, acuérdate que ésta es tu obligación.

PONCIA
¿Puedo hablar?

BERNARDA
Habla. Siento que hayas oído. Nunca está bien una extraña en el centro de la familia.

PONCIA
Lo visto, visto está.

BERNARDA
Angustias tiene que casarse en seguida.

PONCIA
Claro, hay que retirarla de aquí.

BERNARDA
No a ella. ¡A él!

PONCIA
Claro, ¡a él hay que alejarlo de aquí! Piensas bien.

BERNARDA
No pienso. Hay cosas que no se pueden ni se deben pensar. Yo ordeno.

PONCIA
¿Y tú crees que él querrá marcharse?

BERNARDA (*Levantándose.*)
¿Qué imagina tu cabeza?

PONCIA
El, claro, ¡se casará con Angustias!

BERNARDA
Habla. Te conozco demasiado para saber que ya me tienes preparada la cuchilla.

PONCIA
Nunca pensé que se llamara asesinato al aviso.

BERNARDA
¿Me tienes que prevenir algo?

PONCIA
Yo no acuso, Bernarda. Yo sólo te digo: abre los ojos y verás.

BERNARDA
¿Y verás qué?

PONCIA

Siempre has sido lista. Has visto lo malo de las gentes a cien leguas. Muchas veces creí que adivinabas los pensamientos. Pero los hijos son los hijos. Ahora estás ciega.

BERNARDA

¿Te refieres a Martirio?

PONCIA

Bueno, a Martirio... (*Con curiosidad.*) ¿Por qué habrá escondido el retrato?

BERNARDA (*Queriendo ocultar a su hija.*)

Después de todo ella dice que ha sido una broma. ¿Qué otra cosa puede ser?

PONCIA (*Con sorna.*)

¿Tú lo crees así?

BERNARDA (*Enérgica.*)

No lo creo. ¡Es así!

PONCIA

Basta. Se trata de lo tuyo. Pero si fuera la vecina de enfrente, ¿qué sería?

BERNARDA

Ya empiezas a sacar la punta del cuchillo.

PONCIA (*Siempre con crueldad.*)

No, Bernarda: aquí pasa una cosa muy grande. Yo no te quiero echar la culpa, pero tú no has dejado a tus hijas libres. Martirio es enamoradiza, digas tú lo que quieras. ¿Por qué no la dejaste casar con Enrique Humanes? ¿Por qué el mismo día que iba a venir a la ventana le mandaste recado que no viniera?

BERNARDA (*Fuerte.*)

¡Y lo haría mil veces! ¡Mi sangre no se junta con la de los Humanes mientras yo viva! Su padre fue gañán.

PONCIA

¡Y así te va a ti con esos humos! [26]

BERNARDA

Los tengo porque puedo tenerlos. Y tú no los tienes porque sabes muy bien cuál es tu origen.

PONCIA (*Con odio.*)

¡No me lo recuerdes! Estoy ya vieja. Siempre agradecí tu protección.

BERNARDA (*Crecida.*)

¡No lo parece!

PONCIA (*Con odio envuelto en suavidad.*)

A Martirio se le olvidará esto.

BERNARDA

Y si no lo olvida peor para ella. No creo que ésta sea la 'cosa muy grande' que aquí pasa. Aquí no pasa nada. ¡Eso quisieras tú! Y si pasara algún día estate segura que no traspasaría las paredes.

PONCIA

¡Eso no lo sé yo! En el pueblo hay gentes que leen también de lejos los pensamientos escondidos.

BERNARDA

¡Cómo gozarías de vernos a mí y a mis hijas camino del lupanar!

PONCIA

¡Nadie puede conocer su fin!

BERNARDA

¡Yo sí sé mi fin! ¡Y el de mis hijas! El lupanar se queda para alguna mujer ya difunta...

PONCIA (*Fiera.*)

¡Bernarda, respeta la memoria de mi madre!

[26] *And this is what happens to you with your airs.*

BERNARDA

¡No me persigas tú con tus malos pensamientos!

(*Pausa.*)

PONCIA

Mejor será que no me meta en nada.

BERNARDA

Es lo que debías hacer. Obrar y callar a todo. Es la obligación de los que viven a sueldo.

PONCIA

Pero no se puede. ¿A ti no te parece que Pepe estaría mejor casado con Martirio o..., ¡sí! , o con Adela?

BERNARDA

No me parece.

PONCIA (*Con intención.*)

Adela. ¡Esa es la verdadera novia del Romano!

BERNARDA

Las cosas no son nunca a gusto nuestro.

PONCIA

Pero les cuesta mucho trabajo desviarse de la verdadera inclinación. A mí me parece mal que Pepe esté con Angustias, y a las gentes, y hasta al aire. ¡Quién sabe si se saldrán con la suya! [27]

BERNARDA

¡Ya estamos otra vez!... Te deslizas para llenarme de malos sueños. Y no quiero entenderte, porque si llegara al alcance de todo lo que dices te tendría que arañar.

PONCIA

¡No llegará la sangre al río! [28]

---

[27] *And they may yet have their (own) way.*
[28] i.e. It won't cause much bloodshed.

BERNARDA

¡Afortunamente mis hijas me respetan y jamás torcieron mi voluntad!

PONCIA

¡Eso sí! Pero en cuanto las dejes sueltas se te subirán al tejado.[29]

BERNARDA

¡Ya las bajaré tirándoles cantos!

PONCIA

¡Desde luego eres la más valiente!

BERNARDA

¡Siempre gasté sabrosa pimienta! [30]

PONCIA

¡Pero lo que son las cosas! A su edad, ¡hay que ver el entusiasmo de Angustias con su novio! ¡Y él también parece muy picado! Ayer me contó mi hijo mayor que a las cuatro y media de la madrugada, que pasó por la calle con la yunta, estaban hablando todavía.

BERNARDA

¡A las cuatro y media!

ANGUSTIAS (*Saliendo.*)

¡Mentira!

PONCIA

Eso me contaron.

BERNARDA (*A Angustias.*)

¡Habla!

---

[29] *But as soon as you let them loose they'll be away up to the roof-tops.*

[30] *I've always kept my end up* (lit. *I always used flavoursome pepper*).

ANGUSTIAS

Pepe lleva más de una semana marchándose a la una. Que Dios me mate si miento.

MARTIRIO (*Saliendo.*)

Yo también lo sentí marcharse a las cuatro.

BERNARDA

¿Pero lo viste con tus ojos?

MARTIRIO

No quise asomarme. ¿No habláis ahora por la ventana del callejón?

ANGUSTIAS

Yo hablo por la ventana de mi dormitorio.

(*Aparece Adela en la puerta.*)

MARTIRIO

Entonces...

BERNARDA

¿Qué es lo que pasa aquí?

PONCIA

¡Cuida de enterarte! Pero, desde luego, Pepe estaba a las cuatro de la madrugada en una reja de tu casa.

BERNARDA

¿Lo sabes seguro?

PONCIA

Seguro no se sabe nada en esta vida.

ADELA

Madre, no oiga usted a quien nos quiere perder a todas.

BERNARDA

¡Ya sabré enterarme! Si las gentes del pueblo quieren levantar falsos testimonios se encontrarán con mi pedernal.[31] No se

---

[31] *they'll find me as hard as flint* (lit. *come up against my flint*).

hable de este asunto. Hay a veces una ola de fango que levantan los demás para perdernos.

MARTIRIO

A mí no me gusta mentir.

PONCIA

Y algo habrá.

BERNARDA

No habrá nada. Nací para tener los ojos abiertos. Ahora vigilaré sin cerrarlos ya hasta que me muera.

ANGUSTIAS

Yo tengo derecho de enterarme.

BERNARDA

Tú no tienes derecho más que a obedecer. Nadie me traiga ni me lleve.[32] (*A Poncia.*) Y tú te metes en los asuntos de tu casa. ¡Aquí no se vuelve a dar un paso que yo no sienta!

CRIADA (*Entrando.*)

¡En lo alto de la calle hay un gran gentío y todos los vecinos están en sus puertas!

BERNARDA (*A Poncia.*)

¡Corre a enterarte de lo que pasa! (*Las mujeres corren para salir.*) ¿Dónde vais? Siempre os supe mujeres ventaneras y rompedoras de su luto. ¡Vosotras al patio!

(*Salen y sale Bernarda. Se oyen rumores lejanos. Entran Martirio y Adela, que se quedan escuchando y sin atreverse a dar un paso más de la puerta de salida.*)

MARTIRIO

Agradece a la casualidad que no desaté mi lengua.

---

[32] *I'll have no one pushing me around* (lit. *Let no one fetch or take me*).

ADELA

También hubiera hablado yo.

MARTIRIO

¿Y qué ibas a decir? ¡Querer no es hacer!

ADELA

Hace la que puede y la que se adelanta.[33] Tú querías, pero no has podido.

MARTIRIO

No seguirás mucho tiempo.

ADELA

¡Lo tendré todo!

MARTIRIO

Yo romperé tus abrazos.

ADELA (*Suplicante.*)

¡Martirio, déjame!

MARTIRIO

¡De ninguna! [34]

ADELA

¡El me quiere para su casa!

MARTIRIO

¡He visto cómo te abrazaba!

ADELA

Yo no quería. He ido como arrastrada por una maroma.

MARTIRIO

¡Primero muerta! [35]

---

[33] *Doing is for the woman who can, for the one who pushes herself forward (pushes ahead).*
[34] *Not on your life!* (i.e. *¡De ninguna manera!*).
[35] *I'll see you dead first (Better you should be dead).*

(*Se asoman Magdalena y Angustias. Se siente crecer el tumulto.*)

PONCIA (*Entrando con Bernarda.*)
¡Bernarda!

BERNARDA
¿Qué ocurre?

PONCIA
La hija de la Librada, la soltera, tuvo un hijo no se sabe con quién.

ADELA
¿Un hijo?

PONCIA
Y para ocultar su vergüenza lo mató y lo metió debajo de unas piedras; pero unos perros, con más corazón que muchas criaturas, lo sacaron y como llevados por la mano de Dios lo han puesto en el tranco de su puerta. Ahora la quieren matar. La traen arrastrando por la calle abajo, y por las trochas y los terrenos del olivar vienen los hombres corriendo, dando unas voces que estremecen los campos.

BERNARDA
Sí, que vengan todos con varas de olivo y mangos de azadones, que vengan todos para matarla.

ADELA
¡No, no, para matarla no!

MARTIRIO
Sí, y vamos a salir también nosotras.

BERNARDA
Y que pague la que pisotea su decencia.

(*Fuera se oye un grito de mujer y un gran rumor.*)

ADELA
¡Que la dejen escapar!   ¡No salgáis vosotras!

MARTIRIO (*Mirando a Adela.*)
¡Que pague lo que debe!

BERNARDA (*Bajo el arco.*)
¡Acabar con ella antes que lleguen los guardias! ¡Carbón ardiendo en el sitio de su pecado!

ADELA (*Cogiéndose el vientre.*)
¡No! ¡No!

BERNARDA
¡Matadla! ¡Matadla!

TELON

ACTO TERCERO [1]

Cuatro paredes blancas ligeramente azuladas del patio interior de la casa de Bernarda. Es de noche. El decorado ha de ser de una perfecta simplicidad. Las puertas, iluminadas por la luz de los interiores, dan un tenue fulgor a la escena.

En el centro, una mesa con un quinqué, donde están comiendo Bernarda y sus hijas. La Poncia las sirve. Prudencia está sentada aparte.

(Al levantarse el telón hay un gran silencio, interrumpido por el ruido de platos y cubiertos.)

PRUDENCIA
  Ya me voy. Os he hecho una visita larga. (*Se levanta.*)

BERNARDA
  Espérate, mujer. No nos vemos nunca.

PRUDENCIA
  ¿Han dado el último toque para el rosario?

PONCIA
  Todavía no.

  (*Prudencia se sienta.*)

BERNARDA
  ¿Y tu marido cómo sigue?

---

[1] Introduction, p. xiii.

PRUDENCIA
Igual.

BERNARDA
Tampoco lo vemos.

PRUDENCIA
Ya sabes sus costumbres. Desde que se peleó con sus hermanos por la herencia no ha salido por la puerta de la calle. Pone una escalera y salta las tapias del corral.

BERNARDA
Es un verdadero hombre. ¿Y con tu hija?...

PRUDENCIA
No la ha perdonado.

BERNARDA
Hace bien.

PRUDENCIA
No sé qué te diga. Yo sufro por esto.

BERNARDA
Una hija que desobedece deja de ser hija para convertirse en enemiga.

PRUDENCIA
Yo dejo que el agua corra. No me queda más consuelo que refugiarme en la iglesia, pero como estoy quedando sin vista tendré que dejar de venir para que no jueguen con una los chiquillos. (*Se oye un gran golpe, como dado en los muros.*) ¿Qué es eso?

BERNARDA
El caballo garañón, que está encerrado y da coces contra el muro. (*A voces.*) ¡Trabadlo y que salga al corral! (*En voz baja.*) Debe tener calor.

PRUDENCIA
¿Vais a echarle las potras nuevas?

BERNARDA
Al amanecer.

PRUDENCIA
Has sabido acrecentar tu ganado.

BERNARDA
A fuerza de dinero y sinsabores.

PONCIA (*Interviniendo.*)
¡Pero tiene la mejor manada de estos contornos! Es una lástima que esté bajo de precio.

BERNARDA
¿Quieres un poco de queso y miel?

PRUDENCIA
Estoy desganada.

(*Se oye otra vez el golpe.*)

PONCIA
¡Por Dios!

PRUDENCIA
¡Me ha retemblado dentro del pecho!

BERNARDA (*Levantándose furiosa.*)
¿Hay que decir las cosas dos veces? ¡Echadlo que se revuelque en los montones de paja! [2] (*Pausa, y como hablando con los gañanes.*) Pues encerrad las potras en la cuadra, pero dejadlo libre, no sea que nos eche abajo las paredes.[3] (*Se dirige a la mesa y se sienta otra vez.*) ¡Ay, qué vida!

PRUDENCIA
Bregando como un hombre.

BERNARDA
Así es. (*Adela se levanta de la mesa.*) ¿Dónde vas?

---

[2] *Get him out so he can roll in the piles of straw.*
[3] *let him loose or he'll kick the walls down.*

ADELA
A beber agua.

BERNARDA (*En alta voz.*)
Trae un jarro de agua fresca. (*A Adela.*) Puedes sentarte.

(*Adela se sienta.*)

PRUDENCIA
Y Angustias, ¿cuándo se casa?

BERNARDA
Vienen a pedirla dentro de tres días.[4]

PRUDENCIA
¡Estarás contenta!

ANGUSTIAS
¡Claro!

AMELIA (*A Magdalena.*)
¡Ya has derramado la sal!

MAGDALENA
Peor suerte que tienes no vas a tener.

AMELIA
Siempre trae mala sombra.

BERNARDA
¡Vamos!

PRUDENCIA (*A Angustias.*)
¿Te ha regalado ya el anillo?

ANGUSTIAS
Mírelo usted. (*Se lo alarga.*)

PRUDENCIA
Es precioso. Tres perlas. En mi tiempo las perlas significaban lágrimas.

[4] The formal asking for her hand in marriage.

ANGUSTIAS

Pero ya las cosas han cambiado.

ADELA

Yo creo que no. Las cosas significan siempre lo mismo. Los anillos de pedida deben ser de diamantes.

PRUDENCIA

Es más propio.

BERNARDA

Con perlas o sin ellas las cosas son como una se las propone.

MARTIRIO

O como Dios dispone.[5]

PRUDENCIA

Los muebles me han dicho que son preciosos.

BERNARDA

Dieciséis mil reales he gastado.

PONCIA (*Interviniendo.*)

Lo mejor es el armario de luna.

PRUDENCIA

Nunca vi un mueble de éstos.

BERNARDA

Nosotras tuvimos arca.

PRUDENCIA

Lo preciso es que todo sea para bien.

ADELA

Que nunca se sabe.

BERNARDA

No hay motivo para que no lo sea.

---

[5] An allusion to the proverb *El hombre propone, Dios dispone* (*Man proposes, God disposes*).

(*Se oyen lejanísimas unas campanas.*)

PRUDENCIA
El último toque. (*A Angustias.*) Ya vendré a que me enseñes la ropa.

ANGUSTIAS
Cuando usted quiera.

PRUDENCIA
Buenas noches nos dé Dios.

BERNARDA
Adiós, Prudencia.

LAS CINCO (*A la vez.*)
Vaya usted con Dios.

(*Pausa. Sale Prudencia.*)

BERNARDA
Ya hemos comido.

(*Se levantan.*)

ADELA
Voy a llegarme hasta el portón para estirar las piernas y tomar un poco el fresco.

(*Magdalena se sienta en una silla baja retrepada contra la pared.*)

AMELIA
Yo voy contigo.

MARTIRIO
Y yo.

ADELA (*Con odio contenido.*)
No me voy a perder.

AMELIA
La noche quiere compaña.

(*Salen. Bernarda se sienta y Angustias está arreglando la mesa.*)

BERNARDA

Ya te he dicho que quiero que hables con tu hermana Martirio.
Lo que pasó del retrato fue una broma y lo debes olvidar.

ANGUSTIAS

Usted sabe que ella no me quiere.

BERNARDA

Cada uno sabe lo que piensa por dentro. Yo no me meto en los
corazones, pero quiero buena fachada y armonía familiar. ¿Lo
entiendes?

ANGUSTIAS

Sí.

BERNARDA

Pues ya está.

MAGDALENA (*Casi dormida.*)

Además, ¡si te vas a ir antes de nada! [6] (*Se duerme.*)

ANGUSTIAS

Tarde me parece.[6]

BERNARDA

¿A qué hora terminaste anoche de hablar?

ANGUSTIAS

A las doce y media.

BERNARDA

¿Qué cuenta Pepe? [7]

ANGUSTIAS

Yo lo encuentro distraído. Me habla siempre como pensando en

[6] *'Besides, you'll be away (from here) in no time.'* [...] *'Not soon
enough for me.'*

[7] *What does Pepe have to say?* Colloquial use of *contar* (cf. *Hola,
¿qué cuentas? Hi, how are things?*).

otra cosa. Si le pregunto qué le pasa, me contesta: 'Los hombres tenemos nuestras preocupaciones.'

BERNARDA

No le debes preguntar. Y cuando te cases, menos. Habla si él habla y míralo cuando te mire. Así no tendrás disgustos.

ANGUSTIAS

Yo creo, madre, que él me oculta muchas cosas.

BERNARDA

No procures descubrirlas, no le preguntes y, desde luego, que no te vea llorar jamás.

ANGUSTIAS

Debía estar contenta y no lo estoy.

BERNARDA

Eso es lo mismo.

ANGUSTIAS

Muchas veces miro a Pepe con mucha fijeza y se me borra a través de los hierros, como si lo tapara una nube de polvo de las que levantan los rebaños.[8]

BERNARDA

Eso son cosas de debilidad.

ANGUSTIAS

¡Ojalá!

BERNARDA

¿Viene esta noche?

ANGUSTIAS

No. Fue con su madre a la capital.

---

[8] *Often I stare very hard at Pepe and he becomes all blurred through the window-bars, as though shrouded in a cloud of dust raised by passing flocks.*

BERNARDA

Así nos acostaremos antes. ¡Magdalena!

ANGUSTIAS

Está dormida.

(*Entran Adela, Martirio y Amelia.*)

AMELIA

¡Qué noche más oscura!

ADELA

No se ve a dos pasos de distancia.

MARTIRIO

Una buena noche para ladrones, para el que necesite escondrijo.

ADELA

El caballo garañón estaba en el centro del corral, ¡blanco! Doble de grande, llenando todo lo oscuro.

AMELIA

Es verdad. Daba miedo. ¡Parecía una aparición!

ADELA

Tiene el cielo unas estrellas como puños.

MARTIRIO

Esta se puso a mirarlas de modo que se iba a tronchar el cuello.

ADELA

¿Es que no te gustan a ti?

MARTIRIO

A mí las cosas de tejas arriba no me importan nada. Con lo que pasa dentro de las habitaciones tengo bastante.

ADELA

Así te va a ti.[9]

---

[9] *That's how it is with you.*

BERNARDA

A ella le va en lo suyo como a ti en lo tuyo.

ANGUSTIAS

Buenas noches.

ADELA

¿Ya te acuestas?

ANGUSTIAS

Sí, esta noche no viene Pepe. (*Sale.*)

ADELA

Madre, ¿por qué cuando se corre una estrella o luce un relámpago se dice:

> Santa Bárbara bendita,
> que en el cielo estás escrita
> con papel y agua bendita? [10]

BERNARDA

Los antiguos sabían muchas cosas que hemos olvidado.

AMELIA

Yo cierro los ojos para no verlas.

ADELA

Yo no. A mí me gusta ver correr lleno de lumbre lo que está quieto y quieto años enteros.

MARTIRIO

Pero estas cosas nada tienen que ver con nosotros.

BERNARDA

Y es mejor no pensar en ellas.

ADELA

¡Qué noche más hermosa! Me gustaría quedarme hasta muy tarde para disfrutar el fresco del campo.

---

[10] Endnote G.

BERNARDA
Pero hay que acostarse. ¡Magdalena!

AMELIA
Está en el primer sueño.

BERNARDA
¡Magdalena!

MAGDALENA (*Disgustada.*)
¡Dejarme en paz!

BERNARDA
¡A la cama!

MAGDALENA (*Levantándose malhumorada.*)
¡No la dejáis a una tranquila! (*Se va refunfuñando.*)

AMELIA
Buenas noches. (*Se va.*)

BERNARDA
Andar vosotras también.

MARTIRIO
¿Cómo es que esta noche no viene el novio de Angustias?

BERNARDA
Fue de viaje.

MARTIRIO (*Mirando a Adela.*)
¡Ah!

ADELA
Hasta mañana. (*Sale.*)

(*Martirio bebe agua y sale lentamente mirando hacia la puerta del corral. Sale Poncia.*)

PONCIA
¿Estas todavía aquí?

BERNARDA

Disfrutando este silencio y sin lograr ver por parte alguna 'la cosa tan grande' que aquí pasa, según tú.

PONCIA

Bernarda, dejemos esa conversación.

BERNARDA

En esta casa no hay un sí ni un no.[11] Mi vigilancia lo puede todo.

PONCIA

No pasa nada por fuera. Eso es verdad. Tus hijas están y viven como metidas en alacenas. Pero ni tú ni nadie puede vigilar por el interior de los pechos.

BERNARDA

Mis hijas tienen la respiración tranquila.

PONCIA

Eso te importa a ti que eres su madre. A mí, con servir tu casa tengo bastante.

BERNARDA

Ahora te has vuelto callada.

PONCIA

Me estoy en mi sitio y en paz.

BERNARDA

Lo que pasa es que no tienes nada que decir. Si en esta casa hubiera hierbas, ya te encargarías de traer a pastar las ovejas del vecindario.

PONCIA

Yo tapo más de lo que te figuras.

BERNARDA

¿Sigue tu hijo viendo a Pepe a las cuatro de la mañana? ¿Siguen diciendo todavía la mala letanía de esta casa?

---

[11] *In this house there's nothing going on (not a murmur).*

PONCIA
No dicen nada.

BERNARDA
Porque no pueden. Porque no hay carne donde morder. ¡A la vigilia de mis ojos se debe esto!

PONCIA
Bernarda, yo no quiero hablar porque temo tus intenciones. Pero no estés segura.

BERNARDA
¡Segurísima!

PONCIA
¡A lo mejor de pronto cae un rayo! A lo mejor, de pronto, un golpe de sangre te para el corazón.

BERNARDA
Aquí no pasará nada. Ya estoy alerta contra tus suposiciones.

PONCIA
Pues mejor para ti.

BERNARDA
¡No faltaba más!

CRIADA (*Entrando.*)
Ya terminé de fregar los platos. ¿Manda usted algo, Bernarda?

BERNARDA (*Levantándose.*)
Nada. Yo voy a descansar.

CRIADA [12]
¿A qué hora quiere que la llame?

BERNARDA
A ninguna. Esta noche voy a dormir bien. (*Se va.*)

---

[12] Endnote H.

PONCIA

Cuando una no puede con el mar lo más fácil es volver las espaldas para no verlo.

CRIADA

Es tan orgullosa que ella misma se pone una venda en los ojos.

PONCIA

Yo no puedo hacer nada. Quise atajar las cosas, pero ya me asustan demasiado. ¿Tú ves este silencio? Pues hay una tormenta en cada cuarto. El día que estallen nos barrerán a todas. Yo he dicho lo que tenía que decir.

CRIADA

Bernarda cree que nadie puede con ella y no sabe la fuerza que tiene un hombre entre mujeres solas.

PONCIA

No es toda la culpa de Pepe el Romano. Es verdad que el año pasado anduvo detrás de Adela, y ésta estaba loca por él, pero ella debió estarse en su sitio y no provocarlo. Un hombre es un hombre.

CRIADA

Hay quien cree que habló muchas noches con Adela.

PONCIA

Es verdad. (*En voz baja.*) Y otras cosas.

CRIADA

No sé lo que va a pasar aquí.

PONCIA

A mí me gustaría cruzar el mar y dejar esta casa de guerra.

CRIADA

Bernarda está aligerando la boda y es posible que nada pase.

PONCIA

Las cosas se han puesto ya demasiado maduras. Adela está decidida a lo que sea, y las demás vigilan sin descanso.

CRIADA

 ¿Y Martirio también?...

PONCIA

 Esa es la peor. Es un pozo de veneno. Ve que el Romano no es para ella y hundiría el mundo si estuviera en su mano.

CRIADA

 ¡Es que son malas!

PONCIA

 Son mujeres sin hombre, nada más. En estas cuestiones se olvida hasta la sangre.[13] ¡Chisssssss! (*Escucha.*)

CRIADA

 ¿Qué pasa?

PONCIA (*Se levanta.*)

 Están ladrando los perros.

CRIADA

 Debe haber pasado alguien por el portón.

 (*Sale Adela en enaguas blancas y corpiño.*)

PONCIA

 ¿No te habías acostado?

ADELA

 Voy a beber agua. (*Bebe en un vaso de la mesa.*)

PONCIA

 Yo te suponía dormida.

ADELA

 Me despertó la sed. ¿Y vosotras no descansáis?

CRIADA

 Ahora.

---

[13] *In these matters people even forget they're of the same blood* (lit. *even blood is forgotten*).

(Sale Adela.)

PONCIA
Vámonos.

CRIADA
Ganado tenemos el sueño. Bernarda no me deja descanso en todo
el día.

PONCIA
Llévate la luz.

CRIADA
Los perros están como locos.

PONCIA
No nos van a dejar dormir.

*(Salen. La escena queda casi a oscuras. Sale María Josefa con una
oveja en los brazos.)*

MARÍA JOSEFA

               Ovejita, niño mío,
               vámonos a la orilla del mar.
               La hormiguita estará en su puerta,
               yo te daré la teta y el pan.

               Bernarda, cara de leoparda.
               Magdalena, cara de hiena.
               Ovejita.
               Meee, meee.
               Vamos a los ramos del portal de Belén.[14]

(Ríe.)

               Ni tú ni yo queremos dormir.
               La puerta sola se abrirá
               y en la playa nos meteremos
               en una choza de coral.

[14] On María Josefa's song see Endnote I.

Bernarda, cara de leoparda.
Magdalena, cara de hiena.
Ovejita.
Meee, meee.
¡Vamos a los ramos del portal de Belén!

(Se va cantando. Entra Adela. Mira a un lado y otro con sigilo, y desaparece por la puerta del corral. Sale Martirio por otra puerta y queda en angustioso acecho en el centro de la escena. También va en enaguas. Se cubre con pequeño mantón negro de talle. Sale por enfrente de ella María Josefa.)

MARTIRIO

¿Abuela, dónde va usted?

MARÍA JOSEFA

¿Vas a abrirme la puerta? ¿Quién eres tú?

MARTIRIO

¿Cómo está aquí?

MARÍA JOSEFA

Me escapé. ¿Tú quién eres?

MARTIRIO

Vaya a acostarse.

MARÍA JOSEFA

Tú eres Martirio, ya te veo. Martirio: cara de martirio. ¿Y cuándo vas a tener un niño? Yo he tenido éste.

MARTIRIO

¿Dónde cogió esa oveja?

MARÍA JOSEFA

Ya sé que es una oveja. Pero, ¿por qué una oveja no va a ser un niño? Mejor es tener una oveja que no tener nada. Bernarda, cara de leoparda. Magdalena, cara de hiena.

MARTIRIO

No dé voces.

MARÍA JOSEFA

Es verdad. Está todo muy oscuro. Como tengo el pelo blanco crees que no puedo tener crías, y sí: crías, y crías, y crías. Este niño tendrá el pelo blanco y tendrá otro niño, y éste otro, y todos con el pelo de nieve, seremos como las olas: una, y otra, y otra. Luego nos sentaremos todos, y todos tendremos el cabello blanco y seremos espuma. ¿Por qué aquí no hay espuma? Aquí no hay más que mantos de luto.

MARTIRIO

Calle, calle.

MARÍA JOSEFA

Cuando mi vecina tenía un niño yo le llevaba chocolate, y luego ella me lo traía a mí, y así siempre, siempre, siempre. Tú tendrás el pelo blanco, pero no vendrán las vecinas. Yo tengo que marcharme, pero tengo miedo que los perros me muerdan. ¿Me acompañarás tú a salir del campo? Yo no quiero campo.[15] Yo quiero casas, pero casas abiertas, y las vecinas acostadas en sus camas con sus niños chiquitos, y los hombres fuera, sentados en sus sillas; Pepe el Romano es un gigante. Todas lo queréis. Pero él os va a devorar, porque vosotras sois granos de trigo. No granos de trigo, no. ¡Ranas sin lengua!

MARTIRIO (*Enérgica.*)

Vamos, váyase a la cama. (*La empuja.*)

MARÍA JOSEFA

Sí, pero luego tú me abrirás, ¿verdad?

MARTIRIO

De seguro.

MARÍA JOSEFA (*Llorando.*)

Ovejita, niño mío,
vámonos a la orilla del mar.

[15] Endnote J.

La hormiguita estará en su puerta,
yo te daré la teta y el pan.

(*Sale. Martirio cierra la puerta por donde ha salido María Josefa y se dirige a la puerta del corral. Allí vacila, pero avanza dos pasos más.*)

MARTIRIO (*En voz baja.*)
Adela. (*Pausa. Avanza hasta la misma puerta. En voz alta.*)
¡Adela!
(*Aparece Adela. Viene un poco despeinada.*)

ADELA
¿Por qué me buscas?

MARTIRIO
¡Deja a ese hombre!

ADELA
¿Quién eres tú para decírmelo?

MARTIRIO
No es ése el sitio de una mujer honrada.

ADELA
¡Con qué ganas te has quedado de ocuparlo!

MARTIRIO (*En voz alta.*)
Ha llegado el momento de que yo hable. Esto no puede seguir.

ADELA
Esto no es más que el comienzo. He tenido fuerza para adelantarme. El brío y el mérito que tú no tienes. He visto la muerte debajo de estos techos y he salido a buscar lo que era mío, lo que me pertenecía.

MARTIRIO
Ese hombre sin alma vino por otra. Tú te has atravesado.

ADELA
Vino por el dinero, pero sus ojos los puso siempre en mí.

MARTIRIO
Yo no permitiré que lo arrebates. El se casará con Angustias.

ADELA
Sabes mejor que yo que no la quiere.

MARTIRIO
Lo sé.

ADELA
Sabes, porque lo has visto, que me quiere a mí.

MARTIRIO (*Desesperada.*)
Sí.

ADELA (*Acercándose.*)
Me quiere a mí, me quiere a mí.

MARTIRIO
Clávame un cuchillo si es tu gusto, pero no me lo digas más.

ADELA
Por eso procuras que no vaya con él. No te importa que abrace a la que no quiere. A mí tampoco. Ya puede estar cien años con Angustias. Pero que me abrace a mí se te hace terrible, porque tú lo quieres también, ¡lo quieres!

MARTIRIO (*Dramática.*)
¡Sí! Déjame decirlo con la cabeza fuera de los embozos. ¡Sí! Déjame que el pecho se me rompa como una granada de amargura. ¡Lo quiero!

ADELA (*En un arranque, y abrazándola.*)
Martirio, Martirio, yo no tengo la culpa.

MARTIRIO
¡No me abraces! No quieras ablandar mis ojos. Mi sangre ya no es la tuya, y aunque quisiera verte como hermana no te miro ya más que como mujer. (*La rechaza.*)

ADELA

Aquí no hay ningún remedio. La que tenga que ahogarse que se ahogue. Pepe el Romano es mío. El me lleva a los juncos de la orilla.

MARTIRIO

¡No será!

ADELA

Ya no aguanto el horror de estos techos después de haber probado el sabor de su boca. Seré lo que él quiera que sea. Todo el pueblo contra mí, quemándome con sus dedos de lumbre, perseguida por los que dicen que son decentes, y me pondré delante de todos la corona de espinas que tienen las que son queridas de algún hombre casado.

MARTIRIO

¡Calla!

ADELA

Sí, sí. (*En voz baja.*) Vamos a dormir, vamos a dejar que se case con Angustias. Ya no me importa. Pero yo me iré a una casita sola donde él me verá cuando quiera, cuando le venga en gana.

MARTIRIO

Eso no pasará mientras yo tenga una gota de sangre en el cuerpo.

ADELA

No a ti, que eres débil; a un caballo encabritado soy capaz de poner de rodillas con la fuerza de mi dedo meñique.

MARTIRIO

No levantes esa voz que me irrita. Tengo el corazón lleno de una fuerza tan mala, que, sin quererlo yo, a mí misma me ahoga.

ADELA

Nos enseñan a querer a las hermanas. Dios me ha debido dejar sola, en medio de la oscuridad, porque te veo como si no te hubiera visto nunca.

(Se oye un silbido, y Adela corre a la puerta, pero Martirio se le pone delante.)

MARTIRIO
  ¿Dónde vas?

ADELA
  ¡Quítate de la puerta!

MARTIRIO
  ¡Pasa si puedes!

ADELA
  ¡Aparta! *(Lucha.)*

MARTIRIO *(A voces.)*
  ¡Madre, madre!

ADELA
  ¡Déjame!

(Aparece Bernarda. Sale en enaguas con un mantón negro.)

BERNARDA
  Quietas, quietas. ¡Qué pobreza la mía, no poder tener un rayo entre los dedos! [16]

MARTIRIO *(Señalando a Adela.)*
  ¡Estaba con él!   ¡Mira esas enaguas llenas de paja de trigo!

BERNARDA
  ¡Esa es la cama de las mal nacidas! *(Se dirige furiosa hacia Adela.)*

ADELA *(Haciéndole frente.)*
  ¡Aquí se acabaron las voces de presidio! *(Adela arrebata un bastón a su madre y lo parte en dos.)* Esto hago yo con la vara de la dominadora. No dé usted un paso más. ¡En mí no manda nadie más que Pepe!

---

[16] *Stop all this!   How great my poverty, not to have a thunderbolt between my fingers* (to strike you all dead)*!*

(*Sale Magdalena.*)

MAGDALENA
    ¡Adela!

(*Salen Poncia y Angustias.*)

ADELA
    Yo soy su mujer. (*A Angustias.*) Entérate tú y ve al corral a
    decírselo. El dominará toda esta casa. Ahí fuera está, respirando
    como si fuera un león.

ANGUSTIAS
    ¡Dios mío!

BERNARDA
    ¡La escopeta! ¿Dónde está la escopeta? (*Sale corriendo.*)

(*Aparece Amelia por el fondo, que mira aterrada, con la cabeza
sobre la pared. Sale detrás Martirio.*)

ADELA
    ¡Nadie podrá conmigo! (*Va a salir.*)

ANGUSTIAS (*Sujetándola.*)
    De aquí no sales con tu cuerpo en triunfo. ¡Ladrona!   ¡Deshonra
    de nuestra casa!

MAGDALENA
    ¡Déjala que se vaya donde no la veamos nunca más!

(*Suena un disparo.*)

BERNARDA (*Entrando.*)
    Atrévete a buscarlo ahora.

MARTIRIO (*Entrando.*)
    Se acabó Pepe el Romano.

ADELA
    ¡Pepe! ¡Dios mío! ¡Pepe! (*Sale corriendo.*)

PONCIA
¿Pero lo habéis matado?

MARTIRIO
No. Salió corriendo en la jaca.

BERNARDA
Fue culpa mía. Una mujer no sabe apuntar.

MAGDALENA
¿Por qué lo has dicho entonces?

MARTIRIO
¡Por ella! Hubiera volcado un río de sangre sobre su cabeza.

PONCIA
Maldita.

MAGDALENA
¡Endemoniada!

BERNARDA
Aunque es mejor así. (*Suena un golpe.*) ¡Adela! ¡Adela!

PONCIA (*En la puerta.*)
¡Abre!

BERNARDA
Abre. No creas que los muros defienden de la vergüenza.

CRIADA (*Entrando.*)
¡Se han levantado los vecinos! ...

BERNARDA (*En voz baja, como un rugido.*)
¡Abre, porque echaré abajo la puerta! (*Pausa. Todo queda en silencio.*) ¡Adela! (*Se retira de la puerta.*) ¡Trae un martillo! (*La Poncia da un empujón y entra. Al entrar da un grito y sale.*) ¿Qué?

PONCIA (*Se lleva las manos al cuello.*)
¡Nunca tengamos ese fin!
(*Las hermanas se echan hacia atrás. La Criada se santigua. Bernarda da un grito y avanza.*)

PONCIA

¡No entres!

BERNARDA

No. ¡Yo no! Pepe: tú irás corriendo vivo por lo oscuro de las alamedas, pero otro día caerás. ¡Descolgarla! ¡Mi hija ha muerto virgen! Llevadla a su cuarto y vestirla como si fuera doncella. ¡Nadie dirá nada! ¡Ella ha muerto virgen! Avisad que al amanecer den dos clamores las campanas.[17]

MARTIRIO

Dichosa ella mil veces que lo pudo tener.

BERNARDA

Y no quiero llantos. La muerte hay que mirarla cara a cara. ¡Silencio! (*A otra hija.*) ¡A callar he dicho! (*A otra hija.*) Las lágrimas cuando estés sola. ¡Nos hundiremos todas en un mar de luto! Ella, la hija menor de Bernarda Alba, ha muerto virgen. ¿Me habéis oído? ¡Silencio, silencio he dicho! ¡Silencio!

TELON

Día viernes 19 de junio, 1936

[17] Endnote K.

ENDNOTES

A. Suelos barnizados ... y una cuchara. *Floors shone with oil, recessed cupboards, pedestals* [for ornaments], *steel beds — a bitter dose of quinine for* (lit. *so that we swallow quinine*) *those of us who live in huts of earth with a plate and a spoon.* A pointer to Lorca's social awareness: on the one hand the luxuries of the house where the maid works; on the other hand her own meagre possessions (cf. p. 6). The use of oil (linseed oil or olive oil) for stone and unglazed tile floors was common in better-class village houses until the 1960s. Thereafter it was increasingly replaced by diesel oil (*gasoil*). Proprietary varnishes — or glazed tiles — have now generally taken over.

B. ¡Vengan clamores! ... que estaré yo! *Toll away, then. Let's have a coffin with gilt edging and silk towels (slings) to carry it. For you'll finish up just as I shall.* Traditionally in Spain the coffin is lined with black or mauve material and the upper part was formerly edged in gilt. The reference to *toallas* is more difficult. A reliable elderly informant assures me that it was once common to have specially woven napless *toallas* of hemp or linen, some 40–50 cm wide and 2–3 m long, for the eventual carrying of one's coffin. The manuscript indication that they are of silk, omitted by the Losada editors (and thus also by subsequent editors) presumably because *silk towels* made no sense to them, would then point to the specially privileged financial position of the Alba family.

C. Bernarda viene apoyada en un bastón. In all editions prior to Hernández's manuscript version Bernarda's stick is referred to only at the end of the play, when Adela breaks it. In view of its importance as a symbol of Bernarda's authority ('la vara de la dominadora', 88) one has been inclined to see this as a minor blemish which producers should make good on their own initiative. In Lorca's manuscript, however, the stick is emphasised from the beginning, with six references to it in the stage directions of Act I alone. This is the most notable difference between the text of the manuscript and pre-Hernández editions.

D. ¡Vieja lagarta recocida!, *Know-all old lizard!* Bernarda is dangerous because of what she knows. There may also be a suggestion of *brazen* (since *lagarta* may also indicate a loose woman); cf. the association of lizards with heat and Poncia's immediately following remark.

E. ¡**Alabado sea Dios**! In striking contrast to her immediately preceding viciousness Bernarda introduces the litany for her deceased husband, with the repeated response, ' ¡Descansa en paz! ', from the village women. In an Andalusian context the 'santa compaña de cabecera' suggests most immediately the crucifix, traditionally placed at the head of the deceased, and thence, more widely, the archangels Saint Michael, Saint Gabriel and Saint Raphael. In the final words ('Requiem ... luceat eis') Bernarda quotes the opening of the Latin requiem mass: *Eternal rest grant them, oh Lord; and may everlasting light shine upon them.* Notice how quickly the village women's wishes for health and prosperity, as they file out, are succeeded by Bernarda's renewed viciousness. For Bernarda, it seems, formal religious practice has little to do with charity. In context the litany itself should perhaps be staged as an Inquisition-like ritual.

F. **Enrique Humanes.** 'Humanas' in pre-Hernández editions. 'Humanes' is apparently justified by the manuscript and is supported by local toponymy (*34*, 160).

G. **Santa Bárbara bendita ... agua bendita.** The rhyme is traditional and well known in Spain, being an invocation for protection against lightning and the possibility of sudden death (cf. another popular expression: 'Nadie se acuerda de Santa Bárbara hasta que truena'). According to a seventh-century legend Saint Barbara was the daughter of a pagan father who kept her locked in a tower to prevent her being corrupted by the outside world. During his absence on a long journey she converted to Christianity, escaped from the tower and ordered a triple window to be constructed to the Trinity. On his return the enraged father killed her and was himself struck dead by lightning. Saint Barbara is commonly depicted holding a tower and is the patron saint of gunners (*santabárbara, powder magazine, ammunition store* (on a ship)), miners and stonemasons. The relevance of these lines and those immediately before and after to the main action of the play — Adela's revolt against confinement within the house, her excited response (in contrast to her sisters) to the beauty of the stars and the dynamism of shooting stars, the invocation itself with its tacit pointer to possible violent death (cf. 'de modo que se iba a tronchar el cuello') — has been excellently studied by Judith M. Bull (9).

H. CRIADA ms: PONCIA. Poncia uses the familiar form to Bernarda; the Criada uses the polite form. At this point alone in the manuscript Poncia uses the polite form. Mario Hernández scrupulously reproduces the manuscript inconsistency but all previous editors obviate it by changing the words spoken to '¿A qué hora quieres que te llame?' I have preferred to change the name of the character: (1) because the words spoken seem to follow on from the Criada's preceding request for instructions, '¿Manda usted algo, Bernarda?', and (2) because I see a slip with the name of a character as more likely than a slip in the form óf address used. In this latter respect there is one similar slip in the manuscript which, following the Aguilar edition, I have changed without comment: on p. 36, where the words 'A mí también me pareció' are spoken by Amelia in the manuscript — mistakenly in view of her earlier assumption that Pepe left at half past one. Amelia is a heavy sleeper ('Yo duermo como un tronco', 50) and is less aware than her sisters of nocturnal activities. Martirio, on the other hand, is extremely aware of them.

I. Vamos a los ramos del portal de Belén. *Belén* (*Bethlehem* and, by extension, *Christmas Nativity tableau*) evokes religion in a very different context from that of the litany for Antonio María Benavides near the beginning of the play. The emphasis now is on birth, freedom and the innocent world of children (with appropriate diminutives and a reference to the pine branches that commonly adorn Christmas Nativity scenes). But alongside the illusion of freedom ('la puerta sola se abrirá', significantly taken up in the dialogue that follows) 'nos meteremos en una choza de coral' suggests also a refuge from impending danger:

> A la nana, niño mío,
> a la nanita y haremos
> en el campo una chocita
> y en ella nos meteremos.

Se van los dos. El peligro está cerca. Hay que reducirse, achicarse, que las paredes de la chocita nos toquen en la carne. Fuera nos acechan. Hay que vivir en un sitio muy pequeño. Si podemos, viviremos dentro de una naranja. Tú y yo. ¡Mejor, dentro de una uva! (I, 1083)

In María Josefa's song, then, there is a duality of illusion and threatening danger that is exactly comparable to the duality observed in the Saint Barbara reference (Endnote G). It is a typical Lorcan juxtaposition: 'bajo la acacia en flor / del jardín', says the condemned Mariana Pineda, 'mi muerte acecha' (II, 209).

J. ¿ ... **a salir del campo? Yo no quiero campo.** *Sic* in **ms**; all other editions change to '¿ ... a salir al campo? Yo quiero campo', a justifiable change in view of the emphasis on the countryside as a realm of joy and vitality (47). Lorca's manuscript version, however, can be defended and is therefore retained: it is not the countryside itself that María Josefa longs for, but domesticity with freedom ('casas abiertas') which she associates with her own native village, 'a la orilla del mar' (33) — in contrast to this inland village ('pueblo de pozos', 14) where houses, Adelaida's as well as Bernarda's, serve as prisons for the womenfolk.

K. ... **den dos clamores las campanas.** As at the beginning of the play with '*doblar*' so also at the end with the 'dos clamores' we are reminded of the two bells of different tone that traditionally toll for the dead in Spain. Lorca uses a similar cyclic construction in *Mariana Pineda* and in many of his poems.

SELECTED VOCABULARY

The following have in general been omitted from the vocabulary:

1. words that a sixth-former can reasonably be expected to know with all meanings relevant to the text (e.g. **pecho**, *breast, heart;* **orilla**, *(river) bank, (sea) shore;* but NOT **canto**, *song, melody, stone;* **gallo**, *wrong note;* **luna**, *moon, mirror;* etc.);

2. words that are similar in form and relevant meaning to the English (e.g. **espiar**, *to spy on;* **envidiar**, *to envy;* but NOT **condiciones**, *qualities;* **pretender**, *to court;* **registrar**, *to search;* etc.);

3. words whose meaning can be inferred from the context (e.g. **escena**, *stage;* **telón**, *curtain*) or from a mixture of form and context (e.g. **corona**, *crown;* **levantar testimonio**, *to bear witness;* etc.);

4. words that are dealt with in footnotes or endnotes.

At times a word that should be recognisable by one or more of the above criteria is nevertheless included to reassure the reader that such is in fact the meaning in the context of this play (e.g. **responso**, *response* (since some may not know this use of the word); **morder**, *to bite* (since not merely physical biting is involved); **carbón**, *coal, charcoal* (since the context may raise doubts). Elsewhere, where the sixth-former may not recognise a suggested English translation, a bracketed explanation is added (e.g. **orza**, *crock* (*earthen storage pot*); **moaré** *moiré* (*watered silk*)). The meanings given are in all cases those most helpful for a literal translation in the relevant context(s). Asterisked words are not in the text of *La casa de Bernarda Alba* but appear in the Introduction or in the Endnotes.

abanicarse, to fan oneself
ablandar, to soften
*abordar, to approach, deal with
*abrumador, crushing, over-
   whelming
*acatamiento, deference
acecho, (secret) watchfulness
acrecentar, to increase

acribillar, to riddle, pepper, bite
   all over
adelantarse, to put (push)
   oneself forward
adivinar, to guess, read (thoughts)
advertir, to point out
agradecer, to be grateful (for)
agrio, bitter, sour

aguantar(se), to endure, put up with (it)

aguardar, to await, expect

aguardiente, brandy

ahogar(se), to drown, choke

ajeno, someone else's

ajuar, trousseau

alabar, to praise

alacena, (recessed) cupboard

alameda, (poplar) grove

alargar, to hold out, hand

*albedrío, free will

alcance, scope, implication; **dar –,** to consider, realise (the consequences of); **llegar al –,** to grasp the full extent

*aldehuela, hamlet

alejar, to remove, get away; **–se,** to fade into the distance

aligerar, to hurry (along)

alimentar, to nourish, foster

almirez, mortar; **mano del –,** pestle

almohada, pillow

alto: lo – de, the far (top) end of

amargo, bitter

amargura, bitterness

amatista, amathyst

anea, (bul)rush

angustioso, anguished

anillo, ring; **– de pedida,** engagement ring

ansioso, anxious, longing(ly)

anzuelo, (fish)hook, bait; **ir con el – detrás de,** to go angling after

apagar, to extinguish, put out

apartar, to get (move) away

apedrear, to stone

apretado, firm, compact, tight

apuntar, to aim

arañar, to scratch (someone's face)

arboleda, copse, spinney

arca, chest

arder, to burn

arrancar, to tear (pull) out

arranque, impulse, outburst

arrastrar, to drag (along, off, away)

arrebatar, to snatch (away)

arreglar, to arrange, sort out, clear

arrimado, close to, (leaning) against

arrojar, to throw, fling

aseado, clean, spruce

asesinato, murder

asomar(se), to look (peer, peep) in (out), appear

asustar, to frighten

atajar, to head off

atar, to tie (up)

ataviar, to deck out

aterrado, terrified

atravesarse, to butt (push oneself) in

atreverse, to dare

avisar, to send word

aviso, warning

azadón, mattock, trenching hoe

*azucena, (white) lily

azulado, bluish

babosear en, to drool (slobber) over

bandeja, tray
barda, (thatch-topped) wall
barrer, to sweep (away)
barrunto, notion, suspicion
bastón, stick
bayeta, baize, woollen cloth
bendito, blessed
bengala, flare
bienaventurado, blessed
blancura, whiteness
blanquear, to whitewash
bolsa, bag, purse
bordar, to embroider
bote, jar
bregar, to toil (slave) away
brío, spirit
*brizna, blade, wisp
broma, joke; gastar —s to play
   jokes
buey, ox
*burgués, bourgeois

cabecera, (bed) head
cabello, hair
cabra, goat
cadena, chain
caer: estarán al —, it must be
   about to strike
callejón, (side) street, alleyway
cámara, room
camino de, on the way to
camisa, chemise, shift, underskirt
campanillo, (sheep-, mule-)bell
*cancerbero, Cerberus
cántaro, pitcher
canto, song, melody, stone;
   llevando el —, following
   (taking up) the melody

cañamazo, canvas
capaz, capable, likely
capital, (main) town, city
carbón, coal, charcoal
cárcel, jail, prison
carrañaca, rustic percussion
   instrument
casamiento, wedding, marriage
   (ceremony)
casualidad, chance
*celda, cell
celos, jealousy
*cintura, waist
*circundante, surrounding
clamor, tolling, ringing out
*claustro, cloister
clavar, to stick (plunge) in
cofre, chest, (jewel) case
*colindante, adjoining
colmado, overflowing, made
   (fortune)
compaña, company
componer, to mend, straighten;
   muy compuesta de cara, with
   her face heavily made up
conceder, to grant
condiciones, qualities
*confín, boundary
conformarse, to resign oneself,
   accept it
conforme, willing, compliant
conformidad, consent
consuelo, consolation
contenido, suppressed
contorno: de estos —s, here-
   abouts, of the neighbourhood
contratar, to make a deal with,
   hire
cordón, (shoe) lace

corpiño, bodice
corral, yard
corresponder, to be (destined) for
coser, to sew
costal, sack
coz, kick; dar coces, to kick
crecido, puffed up, pompous
crías, children, babies
criatura, person
cuadra, stable
cubierto, cutlery
cuchilla, (cut-throat) razor, knife
cuenta: hacerse —, to bear in mind
cuento: ir con el —, llevar el —, to go tale-telling
cuidar, to look after, take care (of), make sure
culpa: echar la —, to blame

chico, little
chiquillo, child, young boy
chiquito, little, tiny
chiss, chitón, sh-h-h, quiet, hush
chocar, to shock
chorizo, chorizo (highly seasoned pork sausage)
choza, hut, shack

debilidad, weakness
decorado, decor, scenery, set
definitivamente, once and for all, for good
delatar, to speak out, inform
delicadeza, delicacy, tact
derramar, to spill

desabrochado, undone, untied
desafiar, to defy, challenge
desahogarse, to unwind, confide, open one's heart
*desasosiego, disquiet, restlessness
desatar, to untie, unleash, let loose
desbravar, to break in, tame
descolgar, to take down
desfilar, to file out
desganado, without appetite (hunger)
deslizarse, to slip in
desmayarse, to faint
despeinado, with one's hair ruffled (disarranged), dishevelled
desvergüenza, effrontery, cheek
desviarse, to turn away
detrás: estar (andar) — de, to be after (= pursue, court)
dichoso, happy
difunto, dead, deceased
discutir, to argue
disfrutar, to enjoy
disgustado, annoyed
disgusto, vexation, trouble, upset
disparo, shot
distraído, distracted, absent-minded
doblar, to toll
doble, tolling
doble de grande, twice its (real) size
documental, documentary
dominio, domain
doncella, virgin, maiden
duelo, (party of) mourners,

funeral (procession or reception)

*dueño, owner

dulzarrón, sugary, sickly sweet, smarmy

echado, lying, stretched out

echar abajo, to break down

embarazoso, awkward, embarrassing

embozo, (folded back part of a) top sheet, (sheet-)sham

emisario, emissary

empeñarse, to insist

empujar, to push

empujón, push

enagua, petticoat

enamoradizo, susceptible, of amorous disposition

encabritado, bucking

encaje, lace(work)

encargarse, to undertake, see to it, make it one's business

endemoniado, possessed (by the devil), accursed

enfermizo, delicate, sickly

*enfrentamiento, confrontation

engendrar, to beget, father

*enjundioso, meaty, substantial, solid

enseñar, to show

enterarse, to learn, find out, take note, mark well

enterizo, one-piece, full-length

entreabrir, to open (partly), push ajar

entregar, to hand over

envenenado, poisoned

era, threshing floor

escabullirse, to slip away (off)

escalera, ladder

escarcha, (hoar)frost

escondrijo, hiding place

escopeta, (shot)gun

escupir, to spit

esencia, essence, perfume

espejo, mirror

espiga, ear (of grain)

espina, thorn

espuma, foam

estallar, to break (out)

estirar, to stretch

estremecer, to shake, make ... tremble

estrenar, to put on (wear) for the first time

evitar, to prevent

extrañado, surprised

fachada, front, outward appearance

faltar, to be lacking (missing), be rude (disrespectful); no faltaba más, of course, naturally

fango, mire, filth

fastidiarse, to go to hell (blazes)

fealdad, ugliness

*férula, rod, (harsh) rule

fiero, fierce, wild

figurarse, to imagine, fancy

fijarse, to notice

finura, refinement

fondo, background

forastero, outsider

fregar, to rub, scrub, scour, wash up; agua de —, dishwater

frente: hacer —, to face (stand) up to
fresco, fresh air, freshness
a fuerza de, by dint of
fulgor, glow
*fundirse, to fuse

gallo: dar un —, to sing a wrong note
gana: venir en —, to (feel the) desire
ganado, herd, stock; (well) earned
ganzúa, picklock
gañán, farmhand
garañón: caballo —, stallion
gargantilla, necklace
gavilla, sheaf
gentío, crowd
gigante, giant
gloria: da —, it's glorious (heavenly); **que esté en la —**, God rest her soul
gori-gori, dirge, mumbo jumbo
gorra, bonnet
granada, pomegranate
gregoriano: al modo —, in plainsong, in Gregorian chant (tone)
grueso, thick, stout
grupa, crupper, hindquarters
guapo, handsome
guardar, to keep, put away

hartarse, to have had enough (one's fill)
herencia, inheritance
hiena, hyena
hierro, (window-)bar

hilo, linen, thread
hogaza, (large) loaf
holanda, cambric, fine linen
hormiguita, little ant
hundir, to engulf, destroy, plunge, submerge

índole, sort, kind
infame, villain, vile creature
*inquietud, anxiety, restlessness
inquisición, inquisition, probing, prying
inquisitivo, inquisitorial, harsh, tyrannical
instruido, educated
intención, intention, insinuation; **con —**, meaningfully; **segunda —**, double meaning, allusion; **tener mala —**, to be nasty
inverosímil, improbable, unlikely

jaca, cob, pony, mare
jarrita, little jar, pot or mug
jarro, jug
joroba, hump, hunched back
junco, reed
justiciero, of justice
justo, just, (quite) correct

ladrar, to bark
ladrillo, brick
ladrón, thief, robber
lagarto, lizard
lástima: ¡Qué — de ...! What a pity (Too bad) about ...!
*latir, to beat
legua, league
*lejanía, distance

lentejuela, sequin

letanía, litany, long or tedious recital

levantar, to raise, build

ley, loyalty

leyenda, legend

listo, clever

***logrado**, accomplished, successful

lograr, to manage to

lucecita, little light

lucir, to shine, light up, show up (off); **-se**, to show off, flaunt oneself

luego: desde —, of course, for sure

lujo, luxury

lumbre, fire, light

luna, moon, mirror; **armario de —**, wardrobe with a (full length) mirror

lupanar, whorehouse, brothel

luto, mourning; **de —**, in mourning

llamarada, blaze, flame, tongue of fire

llanto, lament(ation), weeping

machacar, to crush, smash (up)

madriguera, burrow

madrugada, (early) morning

maldito, (ac)curse(d)

manada, herd, stock

mancharse, to be stained (sullied)

mandón, bossy

mango, handle

mantehuelo de cristianar, christening gown

manto, mantón (de talle), shawl

***al margen**, on the fringe, marginal

marjal, measure of area; *freely* acre, field

maroma, rope

marrana, sow

martillo, hammer

martirio, martyrdom

***medianero**, between, shared

mejor: a lo —, perhaps, it may well be

mendiga, beggar woman

meñique: dedo —, little finger

meterse, to put oneself, concern oneself, become involved, interfere

misa, mass

moaré, moiré (watered silk)

modoso, prudent, well-behaved

molino, mill

monigote, kid, (little) brat

monte: tirar al —, to go wild, break away

morder, to bite (at), eat away at

mota, speck

mozo, young man, lad; **buenos —s**, fine young lads

mueble, (piece of) furniture

mulilla, (young) mule

mutis, exit; **inicia el —**, she starts to go off

ninfa, nymph

noria, waterwheel

nublo, (storm) cloud

obrar, to work, act, fulfil
ocultar, to hide, conceal, shield
oficiante, officiant, priest
ojalá, I hope so, would that it were
ola, wave
olivar, olive grove
orza, crock (earthen storage jar)

paja, straw
palo, stick
pana, corduroy
pandero, tambourine
paño, (woollen) cloth
pañuelo, handkerchief, head-scarf
*papista, popish
parado, standing about
parentela, family, relations
párroco, (parish) priest
parte: de — de, from, on behalf of
partición, division, sharing out
partir, to break, snap
parto, confinement, child-birth
pasar, to pass (by, through), happen, endure, bear; —se, to get by, manage, do without
pastar, to graze
Pater Noster, Lord's prayer (lit. Our Father)
*pavoroso, frightening, terrify-ing
pecado, sin
pedrisco, hailstorm
pegar, to hit, glue

pelearse, to quarrel, fall out
pendiente, earring
*penoso, painful, distressing
perder, to lose, ruin
*perdurar, to endure, survive
perrito de lanas, poodle
perseguir, to pursue
pertenecer, to belong
pesebre, manger, stall
peso, weight
picado, smitten, bitten
pieza, roll, bolt (of linen)
pisar, to step (tread) on
pisotear, to trample on
plomo, lead
población, town
poder con, to be (more than) a match for, stand up to
polvo, dust; hacer —, to wear out, shatter; —s, (face) powder; echarse —s, to put on (face) powder, powder one's face
poner, to lay (eggs)
porrazo, blow, thump(ing)
portal, gateway
portón, (large) door
potra, filly
pozo, well
precioso, lovely
preciso, necessary, essential (important) thing
presidio, jail, prison
presuroso, quick, hurried
pretender, to court
prevenir, to (fore)warn (people)
probar, to taste, sample
procurar, to try (to ensure)
*propieded, property

propio, appropriate, fitting
***proseguir,** to continue
pudrirse, to rot
pulga, flea
puntada, stitch
puñalada, stab; **tirar —s,** to stick the knife in
puño, fist
***putrefacto,** putrid, rotted

queja, complaint
quemar, to burn, scorch
querida, loved, mistress
quieto, still, calm
quinqué, oil lamp

rana, frog
rato, time; **pasar mal —,** to have a hard (bad) time
rayo, (flash of) lightning, thunderbolt
reaccionar, to react, pull oneself together
real, real (25 céntimos) (multiply by 100 to arrive at today's prices)
rebaño, flock
recado, message
rechazar, to reject, push away
a la redonda, around
refajo, (heavy) underskirt
referir, to recount, relate
refrescarse, to cool off, breathe fresh air
refunfuñar, to grumble
regalar, to give, present
registrar, to search
reja, (window-)grille, grating
relámpago, flash of lightning

reluciente, shining, gleaming
remedar, to imitate, copy, mimic
rendija, crack, chink
replicar, to reply, answer back
resistir, to endure, bear, stand, survive
responso, response, mass
resultar, to (turn out to) be
retemblar, to shudder, shake
retintín, sarcastic tone
retirar(se), to draw back, withdraw, get away
retrato, picture, portrait
retrepado, leaning
retumbar, to resound, echo
reventar, to burst, rile
rezar, to pray
roble, oak
rodillas: poner de —, to bring to its knees
rogar, to plead, pray
***romería,** pilgrimage
rompedor, breaker, violater
rondar, to hang about
rugido, roar
rumor, murmur, sound, hubbub

sábana, sheet
sabor, taste, flavour
salirse con la suya, to get one's own way
sandía, water melon
santiguarse, to cross oneself
segador, reaper
segar, to reap
sentar, to seat, suit; **— mal,** to disagree with; **— la mano,** to let someone feel (the

weight of) one's hand,
wallop
sentir, to hear, mourn, be
upset over, be sorry
***señalado**, appointed
señalar, to point to; **los pies
señalados**, foot marks
siempre, always, still
sien, temple
siervo, servant
sigilo, secrecy, stealth
silbido, whistle
sino, fate
sinsabor, trouble, worry
siquiera, at least; **ni ... —**, not
even
sobrar, to be more than enough
sobras, leftovers, scraps
sobrecogido, startled, taken
aback
solería, floor
soltera, single, unmarried,
spinster
sollozar, to sob
sombra: mala —, bad luck
sorna: con —, sarcastically,
mockingly
suave, soft, gentle, sweet
(perhaps to the point of
slyness)
***suceso**, incident, action
sudor, sweat
sueldo: a —, on (their) wages
(earnings)
suelto, loose
sujetar, to restrain, hold back
sumiso, submissive
suplicante, pleading, imploring

tabernilla, tavern, pub
tabique, (thin) wall, partition
talle, figure
tapar, to cover (up), shroud
tapia, wall
tapiar, to wall (block) up
techo, roof, ceiling
teja: de —s arriba, above
the rooftops, beyond
this world
tejado, roof (top)
temor, fear
tenue, faint
teñir, to dye
terreno, land
teta: dar la —, to suckle
tieso, stiff, proud, haughty
***tinieblas**, darkness, gloom
tipo, looks
tirar, to pull, tug (at), throw;
— al monte, to go wild,
break away; **— puñaladas**,
to stick the knife in
***títere**, puppet; **— de cachi-
porra** *lit.* truncheon puppet
(cf. Punch and Judy)
toque, ring, call
torcer, to twist, go against
tormenta, (thunder)storm
toser, to cough
trabar, to tie up, hobble
tranca, bar
tranco, threshold, door-
step
traspasar, to pierce, pass
beyond
trigo, wheat
trocha, (narrow) path
***tronar**, to thunder

troncharse, to be cut off, break off

umbroso, shaded, shady
uncir, to yoke

vacilar, to hesitate
valor: tener — de, to dare (have the nerve) to
vara, rod, staff, switch
varón, male
vecindario, neighbours
vela: en —, sleepless, awake, watching
velar, to keep watch
velo, veil
venda, bandage, blindfold
veneno, poison
ventanero, at the window, nosy (parker)

vergüenza, shame; **dar —**, to (cause) shame, embarrass
vidriado, glassware
vigilar, to watch over, be vigilant, be on the lookout
vigilia, watchfulness
vista: quedar sin —, to lose one's sight
volcar, to tip, pour
voz, voice, shout; **a voces**, shouting; **dar voces**, to shout
vuelta, turn

yunta, yoke, team (of oxen), (yoke of) oxen

zapatazo, kick
*zarzuela, (Spanish) operetta